EXERCISE BOOKLET

Ann Raimes
KEYS FOR WRITERS:
A BRIEF HANDBOOK

Second Edition

Prepared by Barbara G. Flanagan

HOUGHTON MIFFLIN COMPANY   BOSTON   NEW YORK

Senior Sponsoring Editor: Suzanne Phelps Weir
Senior Associate Editor: Janet Edmonds
Editorial Assistant: Bruce Cantley
Manufacturing Manager: Florence Cadran
Senior Marketing Manager: Nancy Lyman

Cover design by Len Massiglia.

Printed in the U.S.A.

ISBN: 0-395-92643-2

123456789-EB-02 01 00 99 98

CONTENTS

PREFACE

The exercises in this booklet are designed to accompany *Keys for Writers: A Brief Handbook,* second edition. The numbers of the exercise sets correspond to section numbers in the handbook, and the Table of Contents shows the specific handbook section(s) covered in each set.

Instructors who have adopted *Keys for Writers* are welcome to photocopy these exercises as needed; the booklet is also available for student purchase. To make it easy for students to check their own work, we have provided Answers to Lettered Exercises at the end of this booklet. (Answers to the numbered exercises appear in the Instructor's Support Package. Printed on 8 1/2 × 11 sheets, those answers may be copied and handed out to students, if desired.)

Students can write their answers and make their revisions directly on the pages of this booklet; the perforated pages may then be torn out and submitted to the instructor. Students can also work independently, in class or at home, self-checking their work by consulting the answer keys.

PART 6
STYLE AND SENTENCE REVIEW

29–1 REPETITION AND REDUNDANCY

Edit the following sentences to eliminate repetition, redundancy, and wordiness. If you need help with this exercise, see Section 29 in *Keys for Writers: A Brief Handbook*.

Example: ~~At the present time~~ I am ∧now∧ sending you a check ~~in the amount of~~ ∧for∧

      $3.50.

   a. Harold was of the opinion that if he submitted his resignation the group would fall apart.

   b. Each and every candidate for the scholarship must provide two letters of reference.

   c. From the airplane flying in the air over the sea, we could see coral reefs in the blue-green Caribbean below.

   d. The sort of motel we were hoping to find was the kind that had a decent restaurant and a laundry.

   e. Parkinson's Law is a law that states that work expands to fill the time available for its completion.

   1. The house is a gray color with shutters that are black.

   2. I'm not sure that I have the ability to finish my paper by tomorrow morning.

      1

3. Everyone in the bus was given the choice to choose whether to get out at the rest stop or to stay in the bus.

4. In conclusion, what I mean to say is that Shirley Jackson uses suspense in a very effective manner.

5. The United States is known as the great melting pot. It is known as the great melting pot because of the diverse backgrounds of the people who make up this country.

6. The staff of the Museum of Natural History reassembled the huge, enormous dinosaur.

7. We decided to leave the windows open in spite of the fact that the forecast called for rain.

8. In reference to myself, at this point in time, I have a very good relationship with my mother due to the fact that I have taken a good proportionate amount of time to understand her views.

9. I want to become a surgeon. The reason that I desire so much to become a surgeon is so that I can bring health and healing to those who are sick.

10. The committee members worked as a team to cooperate in drafting the aid bill.

30–1 ACTION VERBS

Edit the following sentences, eliminating weak constructions and using action verbs. If you need help with this exercise, see Section 30 in *Keys for Writers: A Brief Handbook.*

Example: I ~~am in~~ favor ~~of~~ prayer in the public schools.

a. There are thirteen children who have signed up to go to the Museum of Science.

b. She wrote a letter making a complaint about the poor service at the post office.

c. We had a preference for taking an early flight.

d. There is only one more thing I have to do before I leave for Seattle.

e. It is obvious that Maurice will not make it to the major leagues this year.

1. There were five delegates representing our district at the state convention.

2. Her piano teacher had always expressed encouragement of her desire to audition for the youth symphony orchestra.

3. There was a small group of students who protested the administration's decision.

4. The former All-Star shortstop gave assistance to the softball coach on weekends.

5. The story was told by Yolanda whenever she met someone who hadn't heard it.

33–1 APPROPRIATE LANGUAGE

Edit each of the following sentences, checking for appropriate tone; direct, unpretentious language; and exact words with the right connotation. If you need help with this exercise, see Sections 33c, d, g in *Keys for Writers: A Brief Handbook.*

Example: We ~~have the capability to prepare prodigious quantities~~ of ~~comestibles.~~

(handwritten edits: *can make* above "have the capability to prepare"; *large amounts* above "prodigious quantities"; *food* above "comestibles")

a. I went to the automobile establishment to purchase a new vehicle.

b. Optimizing their opportunities for profit maximization, the board of directors voted to offer the radio station for sale.

c. My boss shot down my idea, saying it was the pits.

d. While staying in Beverly Hills, they perambulated in the environs where movie stars reside.

e. Severe diminution of precipitation and greatly elevated temperatures are threatening the corn crop.

1. Eating fewer cookies would help me in terms of weight loss.

2. She was admired for her pulchritude from the time she was a tiny tot.

3. When my brother was searching for employment last year, he went to a head-hunter.

4. Most of the money from the fundraiser went to aid the economically disadvantaged.

5. In elementary school, my teacher told me not to play with boys because girls do certain things and boys do certain things.

33–2 APPROPRIATE LANGUAGE

Edit the following sentences, eliminating clichés, jargon, and slang. If you need help with this exercise, see Sections 33d, g in *Keys for Writers: A Brief Handbook*.

Example: The students d̶i̶s̶s̶e̶d̶ ^insulted the young teacher every chance they got.

a. With tires screaming like a banshee, the police car roared off after the robbers.

b. The supervisor interfaced with each department head before the sales conference.

c. Beyond the shadow of a doubt, the novel is a masterpiece.

d. I asked my folks for the car but my sister beat me to it.

e. Our captain tried to get us psyched for the big game.

1. Kennedy Airport was socked in, so we landed at Philadelphia, rented a car, and made a beeline back to New York.

2. The weather was extremely hot and humid from the crack of dawn until sunset.

3. My teacher hassled me when I asked for an extension of the deadline.

4. The manager had a sneaking suspicion that someone had taken money out of the register.

5. The president was bent out of shape by the constant threats to the peacekeeping forces.

33–3 APPROPRIATE LANGUAGE

Edit the following sentences to eliminate sexist and biased language. If you need help with this exercise, see Section 33f in *Keys for Writers: A Brief Handbook.*

Example: ~~Every~~ pilot_{All} must inspect the outside of the plane before ~~he gets~~ they in the cockpit.

a. Each foreman was warned that his workers might strike without notice.

b. All the congressmen on the committee voted to send the bill to the full House.

c. The new clinic helps victims of breast cancer.

d. The Girl Scouts manned the table in front of the grocery store to sell cookies.

e. Off-duty policemen sometimes encounter crimes in progress.

1. Half of the international students in the ESL program are Oriental.

2. A candidate for high office must have a supportive wife and family.

3. The firemen were becoming weary of the false alarms, but they had to answer each call as if it were real.

4. We were awestruck by the Indian pueblos in New Mexico.

5. I don't know if I should trust the weatherman, but I'm heading for the beach anyway.

34–1 NOUNS

Circle the nouns in the following sentences. If you need help with this exercise, see Section 34 in *Keys for Writers: A Brief Handbook*.

Example: Many (nursery)(rhymes) contain hidden (meanings.)

   a.   In the election of a new chairperson, the commission voted twenty times.

   b.   Ben Franklin adopted the name "Poor Richard" to write his almanac.

   c.   Fifty chickens are cooped up in one pen.

   d.   The building's owner wanted to sell, but she could find no buyers.

   e.   Ticks can live for a long time under the skin.

   1.   The Empire State Building was the tallest building in the world for

        years after it was built.

   2.   A general encyclopedia is a collection of knowledge and information on

        a broad range of topics.

   3.   The space shuttle's hull was pecked by woodpeckers.

   4.   I like oranges, lemons, and tomatoes for their taste and nutrition.

   5.   Students could sometimes chew gum in Mr. Norton's class.

34–2 PRONOUNS

Complete each of the following sentences by inserting in the blank a pronoun or pronouns of the type specified in brackets. Some sentences may have more than one answer. If you need help with this exercise, see Section 34 in *Keys for Writers: A Brief Handbook.*

Example: **Each worker is expected to establish** <u>his or her</u> **own**

production goals. [possessive]

a. Myrna is a dancer who knows when _____ is performing well.

   [personal]

b. _____ is welcome at any time. [indefinite]

c. My brother and sister arrived unexpectedly. I haven't seen

   _____ in more than a year. [personal]

d. This book is mine; _____ one is _____ .

   [demonstrative; possessive]

e. Even Roberto _____ could not find _____ house.

   [intensive; possessive]

1. _____ can tell that I haven't had any sleep. [indefinite]

2. Neither of the organizations has written _____ agenda.

   [possessive]

3. Pamela did not want to miss the concert, so she bought _____

   a ticket. [reflexive]

4. _____ time will you arrive? [interrogative]

5. The garden _____ I planted last week is parched and dry this

   week. [relative]

34–3 VERBS

Identify the verbs in the following sentences. label them action verb (V), linking verb (LV), auxiliary (AUX), and modal auxiliary (MOD). If you need help with this exercise, see Section 34 in *Keys for Writers: A Brief Handbook.*

Example: She **could** not **recall** her most recent visit to the doctor.

a. His mother always praised his neatness.

b. Do you know what the purpose of the assignment is?

c. Cheese is good for you, although it is high in fat.

d. The child ran away from the hornets.

e. I know how the money disappeared, but I am not telling a soul.

1. The house burned down before anyone noticed.

2. Please remind me about the appointment.

3. When we arrived at the station, the first thing we saw was our former

   neighbor on the platform.

4. Can you imagine a more beautiful day?

5. He apologized to us for his late arrival.

34–4 ADJECTIVES

Complete the following sentences by adding adjectives in the blanks. Vary the types of adjectives you use. Most sentences have many possible answers. If you need help with this exercise, see Section 34 in *Keys for Writers: A Brief Handbook.*

Example: We were __Confused__ by the one-way streets on our way to

the theater.

a. They had to prepare _____ bedrooms because their

_____ aunt and _____ grandmother were coming

to visit.

b. My _____ dog has been very _____ since I took

her to obedience school.

c. _____ paper was supposed to be on a _____ novel.

d. After a _____ night of partying, we were not very

_____ at the next morning's classes.

e. They had to wade through _____ water to reach the

_____ boat tied to the _____ dock.

1. The _____ money was stolen by a

_____ thief wearing a _____

bandanna.

2. Near the _____ downtown center, the

_____ house stood as testimony to a

_____ past.

3. I bought a _____ postcard to tell my

_____ sister that I missed her.

4. Do you like _____ bread or _____

bread better?

5. The crate was too _____ for Joanne to carry up the

_____ stairs.

34–5 ADVERBS

Complete the following sentences by adding adverbs in the blanks. Most sentences have many possible answers. If you need help with this exercise, see Section 34 in *Keys for Writers: A Brief Handbook.*

Example: The __newly_____ hired operator had a lot of trouble

keeping the calls straight.

a. I had to hire someone to organize my files _____.

b. The painting was a _____ remarkable achievement.

c. The swallows return _____ to Capistrano every March.

d. He was running out of time, so he had to write _____ in his

blue book.

e. The concert attracted _____ one hundred thousand people on

a _____ chilly June night.

1. They found the river rushing _____ over its banks and had to

drive _____ _____ over the bridge.

2. Justin watched _____ as Noah asked his date to dance.

3. The old house creaked and moaned as we _____ attempted

to open the front door.

4. I thought I would _____ hear the words "The doctor will see

you _____."

5. The team closed out the series in a _____ dramatic fashion.

34–6 PREPOSITIONS

Complete the following sentences by adding an appropriate preposition in each blank. Most blanks have more than one possible answer. If you need help with this exercise, see Section 34 in *Keys for Writers: A Brief Handbook*.

Example: We drove __across__ the continent in five days.

a.   The soldiers returned home weary _____ the war.

b.   We looked _____ the edge at the green valley below.

c.   I've never known true peace _____ now.

d.   _____ the long night the mother sat _____ her

baby's side.

e.   _____ the bridges flowed a teeming river.

1.   She approached the airline pilot's test _____ fear.

2.   We could see the car coming _____ the bend but could do

nothing to avoid it.

3.   His parents requested an appointment _____ the principal

_____ his report card.

4.   My sister acts _____ a martyr when she's asked to do

housework.

5.   When the temperature fell _____ zero, we decided to cancel

our hike _____ the mountain.

34–7 CONJUNCTIONS

In each of the following sentences, add an appropriate conjunction and state which type of conjunction you've added. If you need help with this exercise, see Section 34 in *Keys for Writers: A Brief Handbook.*

Example: __When_____ Louis visited his uncle during spring break,

he took the train to Chicago. Subordinating

a. Vera had looked forward to reading the new novel, _____ she

was disappointed that it was so boring.

b. Mark crept quietly toward the deer and the fawn _____ he

wanted to take pictures of them.

c. She tried to sleep _____ the sound of sirens diminished.

d. We can't bring any food to camp; _____ , we will receive

mail only twice a week.

e. _____ visitors lined up outside the museum entrance, officials

tried to decide whether to open the doors early.

1. I don't have time to enter the photo contest; _____ , I haven't

taken very many good photos recently.

2. Some people say that the city should shut down the entire block,

_____ others say that that would be too inconvenient.

3. Our student from Colombia missed _____ her family

_____ her warm weather.

4. Nobody can solve all the world's problems; _____ everybody can attempt to solve a few.

5. Mary Shelley wrote *Frankenstein* _____ she was in her early twenties.

34–8 SENTENCE PATTERNS

In each of the following sentences, identify the subject (S), verb (V), and any direct objects (DO), indirect objects (IO), subject complements (SC), or object complements (OC). If you need help with this exercise, see Section 34b in *Keys for Writers: A Brief Handbook.*

$$\overset{S}{}\qquad \overset{V}{}\qquad \overset{DO}{}$$

Example: In the heat, the children turned on the fire hydrants and

$$\overset{V}{}\quad \overset{DO}{}$$
          splashed each other.

   a. During World War I, Ernest Hemingway was an ambulance driver in

       France.

   b. We gave our plants a good dose of water before our vacation.

   c. The book club offered new members a tote bag and four free books.

   d. The thunder and lightning made the children fearful.

   e. Until about one o'clock in the morning, the party seemed tame.

   1. The embarrassed candidate faced the reporters without flinching.

   2. The pitcher threw the batter a fast ball right down the middle.

   3. Last year the fire department had more applicants than ever before.

   4. Under the peach tree stood a painted birdbath.

   5. The committee considered him the best candidate.

34–9 PHRASES

In each blank in the following sentences, add a phrase of the type specified in brackets. If you need help with this exercise, see Section 34c in *Keys for Writers: A Brief Handbook.*

Example: _Pressed for time_____, we left for the airport without our tickets. [past

participle phrase]

a. At the start of their vacation, they were unhappy _____.

[prepositional phrase]

b. _____, the troops plunged into the wild jungle. [*-ing* participle

phrase]

c. He is a seasoned politician, and _____ takes real effort.

[infinitive phrase]

d. _____, we motored to shore. [absolute phrase]

e. _____, the incumbent governor vowed to run again. [past

participle phrase]

1. The only movie we saw this month, _____, contained a year's

worth of emotion. [appositive phrase]

2. _____, the Southern California coast is unparalleled at sunset.

[adjective phrase]

3. _____, we decided to have our driveway repaired at the same

time. [absolute phrase]

4. Plants _____ will get no direct sunlight. [*-ing* participle phrase]

5. We saw only one sight, _____, on our whirlwind drive through

   the city. [appositive phrase]

6. Working in the evenings, Linda was able _____. [infinitive

   phrase]

7. The children hid from their parents _____. [prepositional

   phrase]

8. They popped the champagne cork, _____. [adjective phrase]

9. _____, Patricia studied all morning for her Spanish exam. [past

   participle phrase]

10. _____ was his only goal after his operation. [infinitive phrase]

34–10 CLAUSES: COORDINATION

Combine each of the following groups of independent clauses into one sentence using a coordinating conjunction or a transitional expression. Make sure your coordinated sentences are punctuated correctly. If you need help with this exercise, see Section 34d, e in *Keys for Writers: A Brief Handbook.*

Example: I don't remember his name. His face sticks in my mind.

a. More people should learn how to use computers. They will play an ever larger part in our future.

b. Marco hasn't turned in a single paper this semester. He hasn't turned in a piece of homework.

c. We could play at the park tomorrow if it doesn't rain. We could play at the Y if it does.

d. John F. Kennedy was president for less than three years. He was one of our most admired presidents.

e. Samantha's grades were better this semester than last. She was happier.

1. January 27 was Mozart's birthday. The classical radio station played only Mozart's music on that day.

2. They have been separated for two years. They have been meeting recently to try to reconcile.

3. It was bad enough that I left the party early. It was even worse that you didn't come at all.

4. Representative Sheehan felt very strongly that something needed to be done about deadbeat dads. She introduced a bill providing stiff penalties for nonpayment of child support.

5. You're going to have to tell the story yourself. It's too complicated for me to tell.

6. Jane's boyfriend always argued with her mother. He generally agreed with Jane's father.

7. Greg knocked on the door for a few minutes. The music blared inside.

8. Death Valley is the lowest place in the United States. It is the hottest place.

9. You may not agree with me. You must conform to my rules.

10. We tried everything to get the chewing gum out of the carpet. We froze it with an ice cube, we poured nail polish remover on it, and we even applied some peanut butter.

34–11 CLAUSES: SUBORDINATION

Combine each of the following pairs of independent clauses by making one clause subordinate to the other. The method of subordination is suggested in brackets. If you need help with this exercise, see Section 34d in *Keys for Writers: A Brief Handbook.*

Example: ~~The~~ Medical professionals became interested in herbal cures.
When medical . . . cures/

^ *they*

~~They~~ began to understand the medicinal properties of many

^

herbs. [adverb clause]

  a. After every heavy downpour, I have to run two electric fans in my cellar.

      The floor and walls are damp. [adverb clause]

  b. The woolly mammoth is an extinct species of elephant. It once roamed

      the northern parts of Europe, Asia, and North America. [adjective

      clause]

  c. The children tracked mud across the freshly washed floor. They came in

      from playing in the rain. [adverb clause]

  d. Local farmers grow corn, peppers, and tomatoes. They sell their produce

      at roadside stands starting around Memorial Day. [adjective clause]

  e. Someone was lurking in the shadows. That person was taken to the police

      station for questioning. [noun clause]

  1. The hikers reached the overflowing creek. The creek was swollen from a

      week of rain. [adjective clause]

2. Professor McNulty suddenly withdrew his name from our short list of candidates. We were forced to begin searching for a dean all over again. [adverb clause]

3. The reporter phoned the editor from the accident scene. At the scene three people were airlifted to City Hospital. [adverb clause]

4. George Gershwin was born in 1898. He died suddenly and prematurely in 1937. [adjective clause]

5. The dance troupe needs to raise more funds. It won't be able to put on the next show without the funds. [adverb clause]

6. The food was delicious. An hour after the meal everyone who ate it began feeling ill. [adverb clause]

7. Some doctors have moved to rural areas. The pace is slower and the cost of malpractice insurance is lower in rural areas. [adverb clause]

8. Our tenor soloist hit several wrong notes. The audience was shocked. [adverb clause]

9. We distributed the meals to people. The people called the Meals on Wheels office the day before. [noun clause]

10. Easterners in San Francisco miss the colors of autumn. They can go to the vineyards of Napa and Sonoma in October. The grape leaves are as colorful as any maple tree in the East. [adjective clause, adverb clause]

34–12 CLAUSES: COORDINATION AND SUBORDINATION

Edit the following passage, using coordination and subordination to improve readability. If you need help with this exercise, see Sections 34d, e in *Keys for Writers: A Brief Handbook.*

Salem, Massachusetts, was a quiet town in 1692. In February of that year, several teenage girls began having odd symptoms. These symptoms included wailing, thrashing about, seeing visions, and feeling physical sensations. They said that they felt as if they were being pinched or bitten. One of the afflicted girls was the daughter of the village pastor, Rev. Samuel Parris. Other girls were daughters of village families. Some girls were servants in village households. The girls accused some village women and servants of tormenting them. They accused some men also. They even accused a child. The accused were brought before the court for examinations and trials. Many accused were convicted. They were sent to prison in neighboring towns and in Boston. By September, nineteen of the convicted were hanged. One man was slowly crushed to death. By April 1693 the witchcraft hysteria was over.

34–13 CLAUSES: COORDINATION AND SUBORDINATION

Edit the following passage, using coordination and subordination to improve
readability. If you need help with this exercise, see Sections 34d, e in *Keys for Writers:
A Brief Handbook.*

Two literary works captured the hysteria of the Salem witch hunts.
The works were written over a century apart. Nathaniel Hawthorne wrote the
story "Young Goodman Brown" in 1835. Hawthorne's great-great-grandfather
Colonel John Hawthorne was one of the magistrates who had tried those
accused of witchcraft. Arthur Miller wrote the play *The Crucible* in 1953.
Hawthorne and Miller set their works in 1692 Salem. They used as characters
some of the real people who had been afflicted and accused. Miller wrote his
play at the time of another witch-hunt. This witch-hunt was directed against
alleged Communists in the U.S. government. It was also directed at alleged
Communists in the arts and entertainment worlds. No one was hanged in the
1950s. Many lives were destroyed. Many careers were ended prematurely.

35–1 SENTENCE TYPES

Indicate whether each of the following sentences is simple, complex, compound, or compound-complex. For complex and compound-complex sentences, identify their dependent clauses. If you need help with this exercise, see Section 35c in *Keys for Writers: A Brief Handbook.*

Example: **Well-known people such as Tip O'Neill and Angela Lansbury have appeared in commercials advertising credit cards.** Simple

a. We enjoyed the rodeo at the Calgary Stampede two years ago, so we decided to see it again this year.

b. Whereas an ophthalmologist is a medical doctor who specializes in the eyes, an optometrist is not a medical doctor but is qualified to examine the eyes and write prescriptions.

c. Unless you tell us otherwise, we'll pick you up at the train station, and then the three of us will drive to the lake.

d. In the summer of 1987, the world's population reached five billion, according to a group called the Population Crisis Committee.

e. The audience for Madonna's concert was composed mostly of teenage girls; the audience for Paul Simon's concert was much more diverse.

1. If we go to the flea market, we must be ready to haggle over prices, and we must be sure to buy only the things we really need.

2. The definition of acid rain may have to be expanded to include dry acidic particles given off by the combustion of fossil fuels.

3. Vietnam veterans who were in contact with Agent Orange, which contained an ingredient that may cause cancer, worry about the health of their children.

4. The seventeen-year locusts swarmed in our area last month and nearly drove us crazy with their noise.

5. The searchers looked all night for the missing hikers, but by daybreak none was found.

6. Flight delays and price fixing have prompted some members of Congress to call for resumption of federal regulation of the airline industry.

7. We nearly failed the unannounced quiz that our teacher sprang on us, but we were sure to at least read our notes every night after that.

8. The dog next door barked so loudly that we could scarcely carry on a conversation during dinner.

9. Within three blocks of campus are two Chinese restaurants, one featuring Szechuan food and the other specializing in Mandarin cuisine.

10. In the Northeast the winters are harsh and cold, but in the Southwest the winters are mild and warm.

36–1 PARALLELISM

Edit the following sentences, making sure that all parallel ideas are expressed in grammatically parallel structures. If you need help with this exercise, see Section 36 in *Keys for Writers: A Brief Handbook.*

Example: In many areas, archaeologists work closely with builders both to minimize the destruction of the past and ~~they want~~ to reduce delays in construction.

a. To be comfortable at the campsite, they wanted not only to light a decent fire for cooking but also needed to have access to an electrical hookup.

b. Tom liked bowling on Saturday afternoons and to go fishing with his neighbor.

c. Listening to the crickets chirp in the country is better than to be bombarded by traffic noise in the city.

d. Dinah could throw a boomerang with accuracy, clean a trout in under a minute, and could paddle a canoe expertly.

e. Betsy was overjoyed and in an excited state when she heard the news.

1. The unscrupulous merchant took advantage of her when he discovered her wallet was full and that she knew very little Italian.

2. In our noontime aerobics class we find people who are present not because they want to be but they feel it's the only way they can lose weight.

3. The teacher was angry both at the students who never did their homework and their parents who never paid attention.

4. Deep in her heart, she knew he was lying but that she would never be able to confront him about it.

5. Phil was an executive who worked long hours and never spending time with his family.

6. The umpire not only ruled that the batter was out but he also threw out the manager for protesting the call.

7. To talk about helping the homeless is not the same as working in a soup kitchen.

8. My brother in Russia said that the weather was unseasonably warm, that everything was moving at a slower pace than usual, and he would be delayed about a week in returning home.

9. We couldn't agree on whether to walk to the theater or if taking a cab would be better all around.

10. The agent told us our luggage was too heavy and that we would have to pay extra.

PART 7
COMMON SENTENCE PROBLEMS

38–1 SENTENCE FRAGMENTS

Eliminate each fragment by making it into an independent clause or by combining it with an independent clause. If a word group contains no fragments, write "correct" after it. If you need help with this exercise, see Section 38 in *Keys for Writers: A Brief Handbook*.

Example: Victor is sick again. ~~Because~~ *because* his internist and allergist failed to consult with each other.

a. I'll be happy to help you. If I have the time.

b. Since 1979, because of a proposal made by the United States. The World Meteorological Organization has given hurricanes male and female names.

c. Because I have the money, I'll go to the concert. Because Juanita doesn't, she won't.

d. I doubt that the author was referring to the Native Americans. Since Western civilization has made it nearly impossible for them to participate in "the system."

e. In my culture, it is a constant struggle for a woman to gain the respect of a man. A culture that feels that women are not as important as men.

1. When it's noon in Boston in the summer, it's 6 A.M. in Hawaii. A difference of six hours.

2. We will try to be ready to leave. Whenever you get here in your station wagon.

3. The incumbent mayor was severely criticized by the local newspaper and citizens groups. When she refused to debate the opposing candidates.

4. The driver of the red car struck a pedestrian and her dog. Then just drove away from the scene.

5. Although Bruce never could tell left from right. He decided to become a driving instructor.

6. *Explorer I,* the first U.S. satellite to go into orbit, was launched in 1958 at Cape Canaveral.

7. At the beach we spent most of the day sunbathing. Not swimming or jogging or playing volleyball.

8. To determine who benefited from the Gulf War. That's the topic for today's seminar.

9. The slaves had to toil from sunup to sundown. Never to complain or rebel or show any emotion.

10. My daughter's goals for freshman year were simple. To pass all her courses and to not gain ten pounds.

38–2 SENTENCE FRAGMENTS

Eliminate each fragment by making it into an independent clause or by combining it with an independent clause. If a word group contains no fragments, write "correct" after it. If you need help with this exercise, see Section 38 in *Keys for Writers: A Brief Handbook*.

Example: You can take the exam today if you want/ ∅r take it tomorrow.

or you can

a. My husband and I always running out of money by the end of the month.

b. Knowing that Fred would be there. I hurried home to see my long-lost cousin.

c. The Vietnam Memorial near the Lincoln Memorial. It was dedicated on November 13, 1982.

d. My brother couldn't decide whether to name his first baby Edison or Harrison. After the inventor or the actor.

e. The lawn needs fertilizer and seed in the spring. Needs mowing and watering in the summer.

1. Tisook said that when she returned home to Korea she'd miss milkshakes. Her favorite American drink.

2. Avoid fragments.

3. He knew what he wanted to do. To win a seat in the Senate.

4. To keep your apartment cool during the day. You should close your draperies and blinds to block out the sun's heat.

5. Disposable income is income that is available for spending. After your taxes have been paid.

6. She didn't report the incident to the police. But slept with her light on for a week.

7. All afternoon, Chan searched the campus for a certain woman. The one he had seen at the dance the night before.

8. Pregnant women should not drink alcohol. Also should not handle cat litter boxes.

9. Reggie Jackson was voted Most Valuable Player in two World Series. The first in 1973, the second in 1977.

10. Jorge hates cats. But loves dogs.

39–1 RUN-ONS AND COMMA SPLICES

Correct any run-on sentences or comma splices. If a word group is correct, write "correct" after it. If you need help with this exercise, see Section 39 in *Keys for Writers: A Brief Handbook.*

Example: Rhode Island is the smallest state, it has a lot of coastline.

         , but

a. Some people love celebrating their birthdays, some people would just as soon forget them.

b. I know someone who has credit cards, she likes to spend money.

c. My mother always said, "Don't run down the stairs," she was right.

d. When we were children, our parents let us sell lemonade in front of our house, times have changed, however.

e. He's not working now he's still at home.

1. Keeping a journal is satisfying, I prefer taping my thoughts to writing them down.

2. Our grandparents watched the Army-McCarthy hearings in 1954, we watched the O. J. Simpson trial in 1995.

3. I have never been to Italy, I'd like to go, having studied both Latin and Italian.

4. The lights went out we started to scream.

5. Some students work for their tuition, that is why they don't have money for clothes or food.

6. Although you may know your way around a car, you shouldn't try to repair major engine problems on the interstate on a Sunday in the pouring rain without tools.

7. She wants to be like her mother, in particular, she wishes that she had her mother's strength.

8. Gymnastics is her favorite sport, she really loves the balance beam.

9. Parents should be loving and caring when raising their children, then their children will grow up secure.

10. Be sure to stay on the freeway until you pass the stadium don't get off too soon.

39–2 RUN-ONS AND COMMA SPLICES

Correct any run-on sentences or comma splices. If a word group is correct, write "correct" after it. If you need help with this exercise, see Section 39 in *Keys for Writers: A Brief Handbook.*

Example: Those flowers are very pretty͵ᶺ^hοwever they don't have any smell.

a. The so-called marriage tax means that married people sometimes pay more than they would if they were just living together that doesn't make sense.

b. Manuel brought the cake, Patrice brought the ice cream, and I brought enough soda for an army.

c. Sharon dedicated her life to Paul, in return he dedicated his life to his job.

d. Last month our middle school sponsored a "TV turnoff," its purpose was to show children that they can have fun without watching television.

e. You need to plan now otherwise your retirement income will be too little for you to live on.

1. In this chapter we discuss the skill of striking with rackets, in the next chapter we focus on striking with golf clubs.

2. For all I know, Mark is still living in Beavertown, enjoying his life, having forgotten about senior year and that stupid bet he made that caused so much trouble.

3. One problem with the free market is that it doesn't take into account pollution, pollution can be very costly.

4. Laws requiring motorcyclists to wear helmets are very controversial they don't make sense to some people.

5. Leonore drank a cup of strong coffee around 11 o'clock, it kept her awake all night.

6. Dachshunds are built low to the ground, sometimes it seems as though they have no legs at all.

7. Chess is a thinking person's game, one mental mistake can ruin a strategy you've spent hours setting up.

8. Jack Kerouac wrote at his typewriter with long continuous rolls of paper, he didn't have to waste time sticking in a new sheet.

9. He did not regard golf as a leisure activity, it was simply another aspect of his job.

10. VCRs are changing the entertainment habits of millions of Americans they are also changing attendance at the second-run theater in my town.

40–1 SENTENCE SNARLS: DANGLING AND MISPLACED MODIFIERS

Edit the following sentences to eliminate dangling and misplaced modifiers. If a sentence is correct, write "correct" after it. If you need help with this exercise, see Sections 40b, c in *Keys for Writers: A Brief Handbook.*

Example: ~~Perched on the rooftop antenna,~~ We we listened to the cheery song of the cardinal/, which was perched on the rooftop antenna.

a. She asked whether the butcher shop that we patronize frequently has fresh turkey.

b. Nestled between two mountains, visitors can journey back to a town that has remained unchanged for two centuries.

c. By the day after Christmas, the children had almost broken all their toys.

d. Sensing that the students weren't prepared, the pop quiz was postponed by Mr. Sanchez.

e. Nearly having finished all the pie, we wrapped the rest in plastic wrap.

1. Strapped for cash, his rich uncle loaned Dave the money.

2. She only saw a blur as the express train roared through the station.

3. To be renewed, the library requires that a book be brought in for restamping.

4. Wrapped, labeled, and addressed, the gifts were ready to be mailed.

5. Whenever affordable, parents in Charlton send their children to private school.

6. To thoroughly screen the job applicants meant spending hours on the phone checking references.

7. While trying to cope with the heat and humidity in Baltimore, my friend in San Francisco phoned to complain about the foggy, overcast skies there.

8. The tremendous blast even surprised the demolition crew.

9. The law firm accepted Stefan's resignation, worrying that he was making the wrong move.

10. Driving home from work in a daze, the police officer stopped me for running a red light.

40–2   SENTENCE SNARLS: DANGLING AND MISPLACED MODIFIERS

Edit the following sentences to eliminate dangling and misplaced modifiers. If a sentence is correct, write "correct" after it. If you need help with this exercise, see Sections 40b, c in *Keys for Writers: A Brief Handbook*.

Example: Greased, tuned, and full of oil, ~~you're~~ ready for your trip.
            Your Car is

a.   The archaeologists almost found an entire dinosaur skeleton.

b.   Costing more than we expected, we could afford only the legal minimum amount of automobile insurance.

c.   The job that she thought would hold her interest completely bored her.

d.   Eager to see Fort Sumter, the tour boat took us across Charleston Harbor.

e.   The picnic table and benches are on the lawn that we just finished painting.

1.   Aware that smoking is harmful to health, cigarettes are nevertheless advertised extensively in popular magazines.

2.   Although his car is old, it almost always gets him where he is going.

3.   Waiting for the elevator to come, a mouse ran through the crowd.

4.   The anthem that we sang sorrowfully reduced us to tears.

5.   Always looking for train memorabilia to collect, our scrapbooks are full of postcards showing steam engines and railway stations.

6.   To completely give up, even though we were losing badly, was not our style.

7. Her beauty even impressed the jaded movie producer.

8. Wandering through the ancient ruins, the presence of our distant ancestors was almost palpable.

9. She only baked two kinds of cookies: chocolate chip and oatmeal raisin.

10. Suspicious of her roommates, her desk drawer was kept locked at all times.

40–3 SENTENCE SNARLS: SHIFTS, MIXED CONSTRUCTIONS, DEFINITIONS, AND REASONS

Untangle any grammatical snarls in the following sentences. If you need help with this exercise, see Sections 40a, d, f in *Keys for Writers: A Brief Handbook.*

Example: My mother asked me if I was going to water the lawn today or
~~did~~ I ~~think~~ it was going to rain tonight.
 if   *thought*

a. Agent Orange is where millions of acres of Vietnamese countryside were defoliated and caused health problems to many Vietnam veterans.

b. Our professor told us to pick up our blue books before we sat down. But don't start writing until she gives us final instructions.

c. The reason the heat came on is because the temperature outside dropped below fifty degrees.

d. The IRS agent demanded that Maureen bring all her receipts for the past year and could she also bring her daily calendar and her checkbook.

e. A handspring full twist is when the gymnast pushes off the floor with both hands, snaps her feet around over her head, pushes off with her feet, and does a 360-degree twist in the air before landing.

1. The history professor told June to hand in her paper by three o'clock and did she know that being a week late was going to affect her grade.

2. The sign said that cars could park in the commuter lot all day for two dollars. Put the money in the slot, take a receipt, and put the receipt on the dashboard so it's visible from the outside.

3. The reason I'm going to Italy in March instead of the summer is because the airlines are offering an irresistible fare that expires on March 30.

4. A bunt is when the batter places the bat parallel to the ground in hopes of getting the ball to roll slowly down the baseline.

5. One reason many schools have changed their dress codes is because students weren't following them.

40–4 SENTENCE SNARLS: FAULTY PREDICATION

Untangle any grammatical snarls caused by faulty predication in the following sentences. If you need help with this exercise, see Section 40e in *Keys for Writers: A Brief Handbook.*

Example: ~~With gypsy~~ Gypsy moth caterpillars that eat oak leaves later turn into white and brown moths.

a. Our desire to climb the last thousand feet of the Mauna Kea volcano made us dizzy and lightheaded.

b. As an African American student who went to a high school in Brooklyn and had a student body seventy percent white, I sometimes could not face one more day in school.

c. In Rita's attempt to appear polite and gracious backfired and made her appear rude and ungrateful.

d. With her weightlifting over the winter has improved Mary Jane's effectiveness as a power pitcher.

e. For all your absences this semester will drop your grade by half a point.

1. The decision that was made to tear down the theater was decided by the city council, not the mayor.

2. With my college education will help me get a better job.

3. When Tina decided to take the first job that was offered didn't realize how boring it would be.

4. When people sometimes twist facts about themselves, such as the places they've been, helps them save face.

5. By writing this essay is to let others know that I was not always the way I am today.

40–5 SENTENCE SNARLS: ADVERB CLAUSE AS SUBJECT, OMITTED WORDS, RESTATED SUBJECT

Untangle any grammatical snarls in the following sentences. If you need help with this exercise, see Sections 40g, h in *Keys for Writers: A Brief Handbook.*

as
Example: My house is as old ^ but in better shape than my parents' house.

a. When Noriaki seems depressed contributes to his family's concern.

b. My aunt and uncle can and have lived for years without leaving the island.

c. All the neighbors wondered how the two boys could possibly get away such a blatant crime.

d. The hothouse tomatoes from the farmstand are as expensive but tastier than those from the gourmet market.

e. The child who wandered into the aisle during the service she was quickly snatched up by her mother.

1. With the greatest anticipation Marina looked forward her graduation from college.

2. The car that hit the telephone pole it was demolished beyond recognition.

3. Deirdre has always but might not continue to have the Sunday *Times* delivered.

4. After a person suffers a long illness is when the support of family and friends matters most.

5. One of my friends who used to work in the factory with me she told me that she could have finished college.

6. She has and will continue to feel feverish and dizzy from her severe sunburn.

7. We prided ourselves on weathering any storm until rained for seven straight days and the basement was covered with a foot of water.

8. Although very few people are attacked by sharks causes considerable panic when someone spots a shark from the shore.

9. Harold enjoys his car more than Linda.

10. My friend Jenny, for example, she applied for a new job recently.

41–1 REGULAR AND IRREGULAR VERB FORMS, AUXILIARIES, MODALS

Edit the following sentences for correct use of verbs. If a sentence is correct, write "correct" after it. If you need help with this exercise, see Sections 41a–c in *Keys for Writers: A Brief Handbook.*

Example: I have never ~~ran~~ _{run} so hard in my life.

a. We had drove fifteen miles before Mark told us about the money he had lose gambling last week.

b. Lots of people have swum across the English Channel.

c. She had went with him five times before her parents found out.

d. She sat the keys on the table with such a crash that it woke the cat.

e. I might not won the contest, but I have made a good attempt.

1. If he had went to college, he would have be a great scholar.

2. Once he got his first paycheck, he begun to work in earnest.

3. After the argument, she did left just as she said she would.

4. The mattress catched on fire because the person laying on it was smoking.

5. She was afraid to rise her hand; she didn't want to give a wrong answer.

6. Arlene bought a jacket that she didn't really needed.

7. If you had took the road I told you to, you would have been there on time.

8. After lying the baby on the bed, he changed the diaper.

9. The engine in my old VW run for 150,000 miles before it finally fell

   apart.

10. I have been froze too many times this winter while waiting for the bus.

41–2 VERB TENSES

Choose the correct verb form from parentheses in each of the following sentences. If you need help with this exercise, see Sections 41d–h in *Keys for Writers: A Brief Handbook.*

Example: **Before the end of the week, we (will draft, (will have drafted)) four versions of our department's budget for next year.**

a. I turned down the heat, but the pie (runs, ran) over in the oven anyway.

b. It is difficult to predict what we (were doing, will be doing).

c. We were having trouble remembering that Na (was, is) the symbol for the element sodium.

d. In Keats's poem "Ode to Psyche," Psyche (embodies, embodied) transcendent love.

e. Leonard (has worked, had worked) two jobs to save money for tuition, but then he became ill and (postpones, postponed) his college education.

1. I bought a ten-speed bicycle yesterday and (forget, forgot) to wear my helmet the first time I (rode, had ridden) it.

2. We had walked out before the concert (had ended, ended).

3. (Growing up, Having grown up) in a city, Leon was pleased when his boss (decides, decided) to transfer him from Milltown to Pittsburgh.

4. If I ever need free advice, I (know, knew) where to get it.

5. As the years passed, we (realized, realize) that we would never leave the farm.

6. I (am, was) just minding my own business when a police officer pulled

   me over.

7. No one (would know, would have known) about the robbery if she had

   kept quiet.

8. When you get older, you will find that a lot of people (lie, had lied)

   every day.

9. If Walter had anything to do with that insider trading scandal, I

   certainly (didn't know, hadn't known) about it.

10. Few people know who their great-great-grandparents (are, were).

41–3 VERB TENSES

Edit the following sentences for correct use of verb tenses and sequence of tenses. If a sentence is correct, write "correct" after it. If you need help with this exercise, see Sections 41d–h in *Keys for Writers: A Brief Handbook.*

Example: We usually combine business and pleasure when we traveled abroad.

a. They will not take a vote until all the committee members will be seated.

b. Some people looked away when they see an accident, but I like to study such things.

c. They were owning the business for twenty-five years.

d. Battles used to be fought with swords and maces, which are used to crush armor.

e. The football coach got so upset by the call that he had stuck his head in the water bucket.

1. I believe that more banks failed in the 1980s than went bankrupt during the Depression.

2. By the time we arrived at the open house, the real estate agent found a buyer.

3. Eunice was going to go shopping at the mall, but the tornado warning was frightening her into staying home.

4. Because we arrived at the party an hour early, Melissa had put us to work polishing silverware and setting the table.

5. We have tried really hard to live by the rules our parents had taught us to live by.

6. The *Mahabarata,* written in India around 200 B.C., contained about three million words.

7. The prime minister left her residence and had driven to the country Tuesday morning.

8. According to Pythagoras, whose theorem applies to right triangles, the square of the hypotenuse was equal to the sum of the squares of the other two sides.

9. Because my parents disagreed about whether to let a baby cry herself to sleep, I have always had trouble falling asleep.

10. Recently, some communities have banned books like *Huckleberry Finn* and dictionaries; history textbooks were also banned.

41–4 VERBS: *-ED* ENDINGS

Edit the following sentences for correct use of *-ed* verb endings. If you need help with this exercise, see Section 41g in *Keys for Writers: A Brief Handbook.*

Example: When I ~~open~~ opened the drawer, I saw the red sweater I'd been missing

for a year.

a. The new edition of the textbook has correct the errors in the first edition.

b. Because she had had four years of Italian in high school, she was able to

skip to the advance course in freshman year of college.

c. After eight hours, he had accomplish his goal of sanding the entire face of

the house.

d. The school committee decided to postpone a vote on the propose

renovations to the middle school.

e. Once the conversation turned to adult matters, Celia excuse herself from

the table and went to her room.

1. Each time they skied down Tuckerman's Ravine, they risk their lives ut

savored the adventure.

2. Nervously she smooth the wrinkles in her skirt before she stepped stage

for the finale.

3. Which is the prefer brand of ketchup?

4. Before I signed up for an eight o'clock class, I use to sleep un' noon.

5. The United States was founded by immigrants and is still being form by immigrants.

6. When I turn the page, I saw the ad for the new movie.

7. Jonathan insist that he was innocent until his mother found the candy wrapper under his mattress.

8. Feeling too much pressure to finish the sketches, Bonita ask for an extension of the deadline.

9. The parents felt oblige to attend the soccer tournament even though the wind chill factor was approaching zero.

10. We were surprise to see so many people at the outdoor concert in the cold drizzle.

41–5   VERBS IN CONDITIONAL SENTENCES AND IN WISHES, REQUESTS, AND DEMANDS

Edit the following sentences for correct use of verbs. If a sentence is correct, write "correct" after it. If you need help with this exercise, see Section 41j in *Keys for Writers: A Brief Handbook*.

Example: He would have done better if he ~~would have~~ studied more.
                                                               had

a.   When the temperature dropped below thirty-two degrees, water freezes.

b.   If the workers voted today, they will not be able to agree on a settlement with management.

c.   She would have known that the butler was innocent if she kept careful notes and paid attention to the witnesses.

d.   If he was sixty-two, he would retire without a second thought.

e.   The principal demanded that we brought a note from our parents about our absence.

1.   If the sun comes out before noon, I would head to the beach.

2.   If you had remembered that I don't like horror movies, you would not have invited me.

3.   She wishes that she went to Europe before college.

4.   I wouldn't live in a big city even if I would have the chance.

5.   If they would have sent the invitation earlier, we would have been able to rearrange our plans to attend the reunion.

6.   The residents wish that the recycling center is open on Saturdays.

7. If we began our planning last June, we would not feel so pressured as the

   deadline approaches.

8. If Sandra gets a promotion, she would move to a better apartment.

9. It's not too late to insist that they would stay until the fog lifts.

10. Our parents proposed that we would wait until we both finished college

   before getting married.

42–1 PASSIVE VOICE

Edit each of the following sentences, using the correct form of the passive voice. If the passive is correctly formed in any sentence, write "correct" after it. If you need help with this exercise, see Section 42 in *Keys for Writers: A Brief Handbook.*

Example: Fifteen trout ~~did~~ caught at the bridge over Roberts Brook one

day last summer.

were

a. The bombs were drop by a B-52 bomber, and the damage was spotted

by a spy plane.

b. The blood samples are been analyzed for their DNA content.

c. After the Oklahoma bombing, donations of food and money were sent

from as far away as Alaska and Hawaii.

d. The audience has stumped by the magician; a girl in the audience was

even turned into a crow.

e. Oval Office conversations were tape by Richard Nixon.

1. After he dented the car for the fourth time, Robert was ground by his

parents.

2. When Hugo complained about chest pains, he was advise by his doctor to

quit smoking and to exercise for at least thirty minutes every day.

3. Live coverage of shuttle launches is provide by CNN.

4. The ego, the id, and the superego were identified by Freud as the

components of personality.

5. Back-to-back home runs been hit by Mo Vaughn and John Valentin twice this season.

6. A live oral vaccine for polio was develop by Albert Sabin.

7. The industrious house painter was hire by three families on the same block.

8. The visiting professor was took to her office and told about department policies by the department secretary.

9. That theme song was wrote by the bandleader for the new late-night talk show.

10. The car has being driven twice from Maine to Florida by the family.

43–1 AGREEMENT

Circle the verb that agrees with the subject in each of the following sentences. If you need help with this exercise, see Section 43 in *Keys for Writers: A Brief Handbook*.

Example: All of the students (go, goes) home for the weekend.

a. Nobody (know, knows) when the new stadium will be built.

b. The coach as well as the captains (lead, leads) the pep rallies.

c. She and I (talk, talks) every day about her garden.

d. There (is, are) five reasons for you to vote this year.

e. Another group of candidates (has, have) dropped out of the race because of the scandal.

1. The district attorney along with his assistants (plan, plans) to attend the press conference.

2. My strong feelings about a multicultural curriculum (has, have) not changed.

3. Because everyone in the four classes (want, wants) to attend the play, we will have to hire two buses.

4. Peas (is, are) his favorite vegetable.

5. A group of us (drive, drives) to the beach every Sunday; most of us (show, shows) up at work with a sunburn on Monday.

6. Here (is, are) the proposals for the new middle school.

7. My opinion of the paintings (is, are) that they are just competent, but his (is, are) that they are exceptional.

8. On top of the bookcase (is, are) my hat and scarf.

9. Several of the students (is, are) doing volunteer service during January break.

10. (Do, Does) the pitcher and the catcher make up new signs every inning?

43–2 AGREEMENT

Edit the following sentences to make verbs agree with their subjects. If a sentence is correct, write "correct" after it. If you need help with this exercise, see Section 43 in *Keys for Writers: A Brief Handbook.*

Example: One of the orchestra members ~~were~~ *was* responsible for introducing the conductor.

a. There was an otter and three whales at Point Lobos yesterday.

b. Her grades is the only thing that matters to her parents.

c. The home unit of the soldiers who were lost last week are throwing them a party.

d. At the start of the movie, from the depths of the seas emerge a magnificent whale.

e. Does the butter and the sugar go into the bowl before the flour?

1. Ethel and her friends Mildred and Alice was shooting baskets when the rest of the team arrived for practice.

2. The sociologist's views of a company man is very harsh.

3. The process of negotiation, coming after months of accusations and threats of violence, were surprisingly smooth.

4. My mother's collection of Wedgwood vases are on display in the lighted cabinet.

5. At the top of the mountain stands several tiny flags, monuments to the climbers who persevered.

6. My husband's headaches always start in his neck; mine starts on the bridge of my nose.

7. Were the fork and the spoon thrown in the trash accidentally?

8. Here is the choir and its director ready to begin the concert.

9. His consuming interest were old stamps and coins.

10. The birds in the beautiful old wicker birdcage sings all day and sometimes at night.

43–3 AGREEMENT

Edit the following sentences to make verbs agree with their subjects. If a sentence is correct, write "correct" after it. If you need help with this exercise, see Section 43 in *Keys for Writers: A Brief Handbook.*

Example: Neither your cat nor your dog ~~are~~ *is* permitted out of the yard
without a leash.

a. Every river and stream is flooded after a week of rain.

b. Recycling or bringing trash to local dumps are recommended for trash removal.

c. Either the sculpture or the paintings is intended for the foyer.

d. For several seconds after the curtain came down, there were neither clapping nor cheering.

e. Several cookies in the last batch was burned.

1. Each doctor and nurse were on the alert for signs of infection in the burn victims.

2. The safety and comfort of the passengers were his overriding concern.

3. Less special effects in a movie mean lower production costs.

4. Neither Pat nor Sharon think anything of walking five miles after work.

5. Her mother or her sisters usually babysits once a week so she can do errands.

43–4 AGREEMENT

Edit the following sentences to make verbs agree with their subjects. If a sentence is correct, write "correct" after it. If you need help with this exercise, see Section 43 in *Keys for Writers: A Brief Handbook*.

Example: Each of the committee heads ~~want~~ *wants* the vote to be taken tonight.

a. A number of mountains in Colorado are over 14,000 feet tall.

b. Either of her teachers were willing to give her credit for effort.

c. A great deal of pain and suffering were a natural by-product of the explosion.

d. The team weren't ready to play, and it showed.

e. The wrappings from a hasty lunch was left on the desk.

1. The equipment for painting the bridges were left on the side of the road overnight.

2. *Rivers of Steel* were printed in big bold letters on the cover of my new novel.

3. Twenty years of commuting by subway between Brooklyn and Manhattan were more than I could take.

4. The protesters who march every day in front of the governor's mansion seek a pardon for the woman convicted of murdering her husband.

5. The number of stranded cars on the expressway increase with every hour that the snow continues.

44–1 PRONOUN FORMS

Edit the following sentences, making sure that all pronouns are in the proper form. If a sentence is correct, write "correct" after it. If you need help with this exercise, see Sections 44a, b in *Keys for Writers: A Brief Handbook.*

Example: Who is going to ask the question, you or ~~me~~? I?

a. Is it okay for you and I to go to the play today?

b. Our lockers are clean; their's are a mess.

c. Albert thinks that no one can jump better than him.

d. For a sundae to satisfy both him and me, it must have lots of whipped cream.

e. He didn't like me singing along with the record.

1. As far as us seniors are concerned, the semester is over.

2. He wants to show the museum to the visiting ambassador and I.

3. I have wanted he to paint the house for five years.

4. My leaving the game early was not nearly so bad as your protesting the decision.

5. Because of Walter, Matt, Mark, and I, we will forfeit the game.

6. I wonder if it was Harry or me who made the big blunder on the report.

7. I wasn't sure that the person knocking on the door was her.

8. The academy awarded trophies to the winner and the runner-up, Sophie and me.

9. Our team members felt that we played better than them except for the last five minutes.

10. The neighborhood has not had it's streets swept in more than a year.

44–2 PRONOUN REFERENCE

Edit the following sentences to make each pronoun refer to a clear antecedent. If you need help with this exercise, see Section 44c in *Keys for Writers: A Brief Handbook*.

Example: She put a can of soda next to the pencil and reached for ~~it~~ *the can*
reflexively as she pored over her books.

a. I got a letter from the bank about a bounced check, but they didn't

answer the phone when I called to explain.

b. In Tim O'Brien's work, he recounts in many different forms his

experiences in Vietnam.

c. After an adventurous first lesson, José told Manuel that he would never

learn to drive.

d. In the newspaper article it says that children today spend more time

watching TV than their parents did.

e. I planted a bush in the garden next to the house; now I just have to

remember to water it every day.

1. Several of Edith Wharton's novels are set in the background in which she

grew up: New York society.

2. When my flight was canceled and I missed my connection, they put me

up in a hotel and gave me vouchers for cabs and meals.

3. The doctor asked whether my life had been stressful lately. It was a

typical cause of headaches and indigestion, she said.

4. As soon as Christina saw Angela, she told her that she had made the dean's list.

5. The cat pawed at the mouse and then it scooted back behind the curtain.

44–3 PRONOUN AGREEMENT

Edit each of the following sentences to make sure that each pronoun agrees with its antecedent. If a sentence is correct, write "correct" after it. If you need help with this exercise, see Section 44d in *Keys for Writers: A Brief Handbook*.

Example: **Either my father or your uncle is coming on the camping trip,**

and ~~they~~ will need a sleeping bag. (he)

a. All students should know his or her locker numbers.

b. In their year-end report, the company gave their stockholders the bad news.

c. Every job applicant is required to state whether they have been convicted of any crimes in the past five years.

d. Everyone on the boys' soccer team is responsible for keeping their own uniform clean.

e. The committee head asked either Joan or Suzanne to use her tape recorder to tape the meeting.

1. All a person can do is his best.

2. The panel surprised us with their imaginative proposal.

3. A police officer must be ready to defend himself at all times.

4. Anyone who thinks they can get away with cheating should think again.

5. When an architect designs a house, he must first understand the lifestyle of his clients.

6. The team gathered in the locker room to discuss their strategy for the big game.

7. My parents grew vegetables in a little corner of the yard. This was sufficient to feed our family for the whole summer.

8. No one was able to finish their exam in the allotted time.

9. Neither the students nor the teacher could find their directions to the theater.

10. Every member of our organization expressed their pleasure at the outcome of the election.

44–4 FORMS OF THE PRONOUN *WHO*

Edit the following sentences, making sure that the pronoun *who* is used in the correct form (assume formal use). If a sentence is correct, write "correct" after it. If you need help with this exercise, see Section 44i in *Keys for Writers: A Brief Handbook.*

Example: ~~Who~~ **Whom** was the president referring to in her speech?

a. Give this book to whomever wants it.

b. I asked the manager whom was in charge of customer service.

c. Who was the director of the student production of *Hamlet*?

d. Who should we ask to play the piano, her or Lupè?

e. She wrote an article about who the coach intended to use in the next game.

1. The professor invited whomever wanted a home-cooked meal to come to her house for Sunday dinner.

2. Whom should I address my letter of complaint to?

3. Whomever would have done such a thing?

4. Who did you appoint to run the meeting in your absence?

5. I forgot to tell you whom would not be going on the trip.

45–1 ADJECTIVES AND ADVERBS

Edit the following sentences to correct any errors in the use of adjectives and adverbs. If a sentence is correct, write "correct" after it. If you need help with this exercise, see Section 45 in *Keys for Writers: A Brief Handbook.*

Example: If you're not ~~real~~ really sick, you'll have to take the test.

a. If you don't do good on the test, you may have to repeat the course.

b. He acted so unreasonable that we had to leave the party early.

c. She darted quick between the opposing players and then dribbled swift for the basket.

d. They couldn't scarcely contain their excitement on arriving in Rome.

e. The moon did not appear very brightly even though it was full tonight.

1. He felt pretty good until he heard the news; then he looked terribly.

2. The officer wrongly assumed that I had been parked illegally.

3. The senator felt badly about not getting enough votes to pass the aid bill for her constituents.

4. She looked very prettily, all ready for the wedding.

5. After near failing the pop quiz, the students spent considerable more time studying for the next test.

6. I never spend no money on lottery tickets.

7. My grandmother has some old-fashion ideas, but she also feels very openly to new ideas.

8. The shirt was obviously made cheap, but it looked similarly to the one with the designer label.

9. Treading careful and slow, the campers crossed the creek on the fallen log.

10. She told the child that if he would sit quiet while she was gone, they would take a real long walk when she returned.

45–2 PLACEMENT OF ADJECTIVES AND ADVERBS

Edit the following sentences, making sure that adjectives and adverbs are correctly placed and punctuated. If you need help with this exercise, see Sections 45e, f in *Keys for Writers: A Brief Handbook*.

Example: We cooked ⌐quickly¬ the dinner.

a. When we pulled into the lot we saw many red expensive cars, but we were looking for a white inexpensive car.

b. The buttons perfectly were sewn onto the sweater.

c. To cheer me up on this dreary day, I brought along my new flowered huge umbrella.

d. The rain steadily fell throughout the day.

e. The green nondescript abandoned building on the corner is being turned into a gray Catholic little church.

1. My older brother made a wooden comfortable tree house when he was in the eighth grade.

2. On our street lives a family of five black enormous crows.

3. I'm looking forward to living in England, but I'm not looking forward to many cold damp days.

4. The realtor sold promptly the brick yellow house.

5. She organized her library by size and color: the paperback blue large books on one shelf, the hardcover small green books on another, and so on.

45–3 COMPARATIVE AND SUPERLATIVE FORMS OF ADJECTIVES AND ADVERBS

Edit the following sentences, eliminating any problems with the form or use of adjectives and adverbs. If a sentence is correct, write "correct" after it. If you need help with this exercise, see Section 45h in *Keys for Writers: A Brief Handbook.*

Example: Of the students in our class, Mildred was the ~~better~~ best speller.

a. He claimed that his expensive new shoes helped him to run more quicklier than he'd ever run before.

b. The largest of my feet is a full half-inch longer than the smallest.

c. Henry's painting is good, but Amy's is even more better.

d. No one could feel worser than I feel today.

e. My sister and I were always competitive, but we reached a silent agreement: she was more pretty but I was more smarter.

1. Elvira grew so tall that soon she was the most tallest girl on the block.

2. The sign said that we shouldn't drive slowlier than 45 mph on the interstate.

3. The candidate who spoke last was the most reasonable of all five candidates.

4. My dog is lesser dangerous than the one next door, but the one around the corner is the least dangerous of all.

5. Martin decided that if he exercised all summer and didn't eat too much junk food, he would be more stronger than any other student trying out for the football team.

6. My mother asked me to taste two versions of brownies; I couldn't really say that I liked one better than the other.

7. Don't you agree that Dr. Zimian is more qualified to run the new outpatient clinic?

8. That was the most easy assignment we've ever had to do.

9. Cindy always thought that her drawings were more colorful.

10. Aaron felt stronglier than Josephine about the company's human rights violations, and he organized a massive boycott of the company's products.

45–4 FAULTY OR INCOMPLETE COMPARISONS

Edit the following sentences to eliminate faulty or incomplete comparisons. If a sentence is correct, write "correct" after it. If you need help with this exercise, see Section 45i in *Keys for Writers: A Brief Handbook*.

Example: She likes traveling better than her husband does.

a. Joanna's pet fish has ore fins than her boyfriend.

b. Jake walks his own dog more often than his son.

c. Celia wants a vacation more than her fiancé.

d. Julia's paper received a better grade than Mark's.

e. The review said the famous director's new movie was more violent.

1. Our waiter said today's stew had more carrots than yesterday.

2. The playwright wrote as many plays as Shakespeare.

3. Helen wants her hair cut as short as Jill.

4. Bob likes bowling better than flying.

5. Madelaine likes to color better than her sister.

46–1 RELATIVE CLAUSES AND RELATIVE PRONOUNS

Edit the following sentences to eliminate problems in the use of relative clauses (assume formal use). If a sentence is correct, write "correct" after it. If you need help with this exercise, see Section 46 in *Keys for Writers: A Brief Handbook.*

Example: The person ~~who~~ *whom* you elect will serve as president for three years.

a. We ordered trophies for all the players whom we feel deserve recognition.

b. We always prefer to debate with people who expresses themselves forcefully.

c. Runners which stretch before they run have fewer injuries than those which don't stretch.

d. The book whose cover is torn has been checked out of the library continuously since it was placed on the shelf.

e. One of the violinists who plays in the pops orchestra will be selected to join the symphony orchestra at the end of the season.

1. Javier wrote the letter to the official whom he understood was in charge of monitoring employment abuses.

2. The only one of the plants that have bloomed this year is the one closest to the house.

3. The picnickers who the ants annoyed moved three times before packing up and going home.

4. The ballplayers voted for the umpires who they felt called the fairest game.

5. The graduating class honored the priest whose center for the homeless has become a national model.

46–2 RELATIVE CLAUSES AND RELATIVE PRONOUNS

Edit the following sentences to correct any mistakes in the wording or punctuation of relative clauses. (The prompts in brackets give necessary information about some sentence elements.) If a sentence is correct, write "correct" after it. If you need help with this exercise, see Section 46 in *Keys for Writers: A Brief Handbook.*

Example: The contract, ~~which~~ *that* he signed hours before his death, will

guarantee a large inheritance to his sons and daughters. [He

signed more than one contract in his lifetime.]

a. My mother who has worked all her life will finally retire in July.

b. The paper, which we were assigned on October 10, is due on November

10. [We were assigned more than one paper.]

c. The word *awesome* that I use all the time does not really mean

"interesting" or "cool."

d. The counselor to which I referred my brother was kind enough to find

time in her schedule for him.

e. Students, who study every day, fare better on tests than students, who

cram the night before.

1. She spent her time entering data into the computer that were sent in by

agents all over the country.

2. The grant, which Jillian received, will provide her with a modest stipend

so she can continue her research. [There are other grants and other

applicants.]

3. The novel, that is written in French, is more complicated than the musical and not nearly as enjoyable.

4. The hours of the after-school program are meant to accommodate children, whose parents work.

5. The proposal called for adding three trains to the schedule that would travel express between Providence and New Haven.

6. Sara's cousin that lived with her in the summer she has decided to apply to medical school and get hesr own apartment. [Sara has more than one cousin.]

7. The thing what she hoped for most was a few days' rest before starting her concert tour.

8. Mauna Kea, which is the highest peak in Hawaii, is an extinct volcano.

9. The lawyer to which I directed my letter he was the only one who knew about the divorce codes.

10. The interns which most of them we hired at the beginning of the summer ended up staying on full-time in the fall.

PART 8
PUNCTUATION, MECHANICS, AND SPELLING

47–1 COMMAS: COORDINATION, INTRODUCTORY ELEMENTS

Add commas where they are needed in the following sentences. If a sentence is correct, write "correct" after it. If you need help with this exercise, see Sections 47a–c in *Keys for Writers: A Brief Handbook.*

Example: Because the plane was late leaving O'Hare, we missed our

connection.

a. Unlike the national security adviser the senator believed that the

president needed a full accounting of events.

b. She does not know who her secret admirer is but she appreciates the

attention.

c. Wearing a beaded collar the poodle pranced around the ring.

d. After mowing and trimming the lawn looked like a velvet carpet.

e. He hated the crowds, and he resented the long drive home.

1. When you finish reading the book you should return it to the library right

away.

2. Before the Pilgrims arrived at Plymouth they landed at Provincetown,

on the tip of Cape Cod.

3. Donna had a cold so she did not attend the baby's first birthday party.

82

4. Mary did not want to hurt John's feelings yet she could not break her date.

5. Marvin's cousin mowed the lawn and his sister weeded the garden.

6. Beyond the river the fields sloped gently toward the woods.

7. Because we could read neither Spanish nor Portuguese we signed up for a literature course in Latin American writers in translation.

8. According to the study teenage boys who watched four or more hours of television were less physically fit than boys who watched less television.

9. To prepare for our stay in the Philippines we tried to teach ourselves Tagalog but we had to admit defeat and find a teacher to help us.

10. If smoking is harmful to our health why aren't cigarette ads illegal?

47–2   COMMAS: NONRESTRICTIVE ELEMENTS
AND TRANSITIONAL EXPRESSIONS

Add commas where they are needed in the following sentences. If a sentence is correct, write "correct" after it. If you need help with this exercise, see Sections 47d, e in *Keys for Writers: A Brief Handbook*.

Example: At the National Museum of American History, which is part of

the Smithsonian Institution, we were very moved by the exhibit

"Offerings at the Wall."

a.   Alaska the forty-ninth state and Hawaii the fiftieth were both admitted to the Union in 1959.

b.   We continue to assert however that dogs abandoned by their owners should first be offered to the public for adoption.

c.   John Wesley Powell who led geological expeditions into Colorado and Utah had lost an arm during the Civil War.

d.   Nevertheless he decided to brave the storm and drive home.

e.   Athletes who avoid fitness training will be dropped from the intramural and intercollegiate teams.

1.   That man in the green shirt is the one who tipped over the garbage can.

2.   Janet Munro who began singing at the age of three received her first starring role just last year.

3.   Harold was not accustomed furthermore to being ignored.

4.   Of course we only wanted to set the record straight.

5.   Maria enjoying her brief vacation did nothing all day but sleep and read.

47–3 COMMAS: MISCELLANEOUS USES

Add commas where they are needed in the following sentences. If a sentence is correct, write "correct" after it. If you need help with this exercise, see Sections 47f–j in *Keys for Writers: A Brief Handbook*.

Example: My schedule next year includes American government, biology, calculus, and intermediate Italian.

a. It was a hot smoggy and depressing day.

b. I opened the door looked around the room and finally spotted the raincoat I'd forgotten.

c. December 7 1941 was the date that President Roosevelt said would "live in infamy."

d. The moldy, dank smell in the cellar was caused by porous walls that leaked whenever it rained.

e. Joan Bergmann LL.D. opened her solo office as soon as she graduated from law school.

1. The new employee said that he lived at 2199 Davidson Drive Des Moines Iowa.

2. "If you trust me" she said "you will do as I say."

3. The large gray house was set back from the busy street.

4. I grew up in Cincinnati Ohio and my college roommate grew up not far away in Covington Kentucky.

5. The dirty mangy mutt followed the frightened six-year-old child home.

6. "Yes, you may have two more days to complete your paper" said Professor Herrera.

7. Why can't we spend a few days in Naples, Venice and Rome?

8. We couldn't decide whether to mow the lawn to clean the attic or to go to the beach.

9. How will we decide whether to pay $25,500 for the sporty red car or $22,000 for the sensible family sedan?

10. For the barbecue John assembled beef chunks, whole onions green peppers, tomatoes and mushrooms.

47–4 COMMAS: MISUSES

Add commas where they are needed in the following sentences, and delete unnecessary commas. If a sentence is correct, write "correct" after it. If you need help with this exercise, see Section 47i in *Keys for Writers: A Brief Handbook.*

Example: A major deterrent to the exploration/ and settlement of Mars/ is

lack of water.

a. We should not necessarily think, that he is the one to blame.

b. Eleven, very tired Brownies, and their adult leaders were happy to go
   home after the overnight camping trip.

c. She had three interviews in three hours, and she was very happy about her
   prospects.

d. Dixie, Peanuts, and Clement, were what we called the puppies.

e. There are too many tomatoes in the soup, and not enough carrots.

1. It rained on Wednesday, and snowed on Thursday.

2. Lionel tried to find his keys and even took the backseat out of his car.

3. The statistician, who designed the test, wrote about her technique in this
   month's journal.

4. He excused himself, and hastily left the room.

5. The old, oak tree was a stately presence in the overcrowded,
   neighborhood.

6. The maître d' welcomed valued customers with a polite, understated, bow, and unfamiliar customers with a curt smile.

7. The child grinned sheepishly as he squashed, the long-legged, spider.

8. I shoveled the snow all day but, I didn't get from one end of the driveway to the other.

9. I returned my seriously overdue book to the library, and couldn't resist checking out two more.

10. My sister uprooted many plants such as, pansies, tulips, yews, and even poison ivy.

48–1 APOSTROPHES

Add apostrophes where they are needed and delete apostrophes used incorrectly in the following sentences. (The prompts in brackets give necessary information about some sentence elements.) If a sentence is correct, write "correct" after it. If you need help with this exercise, see Section 48 in *Keys for Writers: A Brief Handbook*.

Example: There's a place down the road where you're welcome anytime.

a. Ill sew the costumes if youll paint the sets.

b. Sarah liked to look at her brothers's record album covers from the 60's. [Sarah has more than one brother.]

c. My sister-in-laws house is more than 150 years old; it's most interesting feature is a hidden passageway in the library.

d. When we visited Ireland, we tried to locate the Murphy's, who used to live next door to us.

e. Their house is on the sunny side of the street; our's is on the shady side.

1. Veronica has always had problems' with her nieces' daughter.

2. The childrens' clothing was soaked from the unexpected downpour.

3. After sixteen years Silas's gold was found.

4. I don't know how many As I have to get on my report card to please my parents.

5. Little Andrew insisted on pulling the gooses tail.

49–1 QUOTATION MARKS

Add quotation marks as needed in the following sentences and delete unnecessary quotation marks. Make sure that punctuation is used correctly with the quotation marks. If you need help with this exercise, see Section 49 in *Keys for Writers: A Brief Handbook.*

Example: "Why," my mother asked me, "do all your friends call you Big

Moe?"

a. Why were we assigned Poe's story The Tell-Tale Heart?

b. The judge asked "whether the jury had reached a verdict."

c. Our parents used to think that lyrics like I want to hold your hand were

profound.

d. I think that I shall never see / a billboard lovely as a tree Ogden Nash

wrote, in parody of Joyce Kilmer's poem Trees.

e. The teacher asked, Who said, Give me liberty or give me death?

1. It was George Herman Ruth's prodigious home run hitting that earned

him the nickname Sultan of Swat.

2. In *The Wizard of Oz,* Dorothy says There's no place like home, but most

viewers leave the movie singing Ding dong the wicked witch is dead.

3. Sonya in Chekhov's *Uncle Vanya* says, When a woman isn't beautiful,

people always say, "You have lovely eyes, you have lovely hair."

4. About his expectations for Americans, John F. Kennedy was very clear, Ask not what your country can do for you—ask what you can do for your country.

5. In the poem Maul Muller, John Greenleaf Whittier wrote, "For all words of tongue or pen, / The saddest are these: "It might have been"."

50–1   SEMICOLONS

Add, replace, or remove semicolons as appropriate in the following sentences. If a sentence is correct, write "correct" after it. If you need help with this exercise, see Section 50 in *Keys for Writers: A Brief Handbook.*

Example: It may rain tomorrow, however, we will go on a picnic anyway.

a. Mary has lived in many places: Worcester, Massachusetts, Newark, New Jersey, Charleston, South Carolina, and Miami, Florida.

b. It snowed very little that winter, nevertheless, sales of ski equipment soared.

c. True friends exhibit four main qualities; openness, trust, loyalty, and love.

d. The county's water shortage was severe; many restaurants in the area stopped serving water with meals unless a customer specifically requested it.

e. The president is going to veto the bill; at least he said he would.

1. Learn your students' names as soon as you can, take an interest in them as individuals.

2. My grandmother always insisted that we eat every last scrap on our plates; she had grown up in the Depression and remembered going hungry many nights.

3. Although the wind was fierce and the temperature had fallen steadily all night; the sailing party held to its plan of leaving at dawn.

4. It was feeding time at the zoo; the zookeepers fed the animals in the African exhibit first.

5. To unwind after our last exam, we spent an evening watching old romantic comedies: *Philadelphia Story,* starring Katharine Hepburn, Cary Grant, and James Stewart, *Roman Holiday,* with Audrey Hepburn and Gregory Peck, and the all-time classic *Casablanca,* with Humphrey Bogart and Ingrid Bergman.

51–1 PERIODS, QUESTION MARKS, AND EXCLAMATION POINTS

Add or delete periods, question marks, and exclamation points as appropriate in the following sentences. If a sentence is correct, write "correct" after it. If you need help with this exercise, see Section 51a in *Keys for Writers: A Brief Handbook.*

Example: I wonder when spring will come.

a. Would you please give me a call as soon as you're ready

b. "Are you crazy" he asked

c. "The tornado is heading straight for us" he screamed. "Run for your life"

d. My younger sister spent a week at a space camp run by N.A.S.A.

e. With parents like that, is it any wonder that he's always late

1. I keep pondering what's beyond the end of the universe

2. Will you be staying with us this evening

3. I asked Milt if he really wanted me to withdraw his name from consideration

4. We were all proud of Uncle Jerry, who at the age of thirty-seven had finally earned his B.A.

5. Why didn't I think of that

51–2 COLONS

Add, replace, or remove colons as appropriate in the following sentences. If a sentence is correct, write "correct" after it. If you need help with this exercise, see Section 51b in *Keys for Writers: A Brief Handbook*.

Example: At the stationery store, we need: pencils pens, notepaper,

folders, and labels.

a. His plan was obvious, break the window, cut the wires, snatch the jewels,

and sneak down the fire escape.

b. My favorite Gospel story is that of the Samaritan woman at the well in

John 4,9–30.

c. For her driving test, Monica hoped for: a kind inspector, no yellow

lights, no oncoming traffic, and no empty parking spots for parallel

parking.

d. John was ready to go to his job interview, but there was one small

problem; he couldn't find his car keys.

e. The effects of sleep deprivation include listlessness, irritability, and an

inability to concentrate.

1. That airline serves many Asian cities, including: Tokyo, Beijing, Hong

Kong, and Seoul.

2. Management made one big concession; the company would continue to

pay all employees' health insurance premiums.

3. To restore profits, the consultant recommended three actions: cut employee wages, increase advertising, and eliminate stock options.

4. Two anticipated effects of the storm were: increased erosion of the shoreline and a flash flood in the center of town.

5. The movie had a disappointing ending; the hero joined the villains.

51–3 DASHES, PARENTHESES, BRACKETS, SLASHES, AND ELLIPSIS DOTS

In the following sentences, punctuate the italicized words (and the spaces around and between them) appropriately, using dashes, parentheses, brackets, slashes, or ellipsis dots. (The prompts in brackets give necessary information about some sentences.) If you need help with this exercise, see Sections 51c–g in *Keys for Writers: A Brief Handbook.*

Example: The heroes of my parents' youth —*John F. Kennedy, for example*— seem somehow more heroic than the heroes of my generation.

a. Vice President Richard Nixon *who later became the thirty-seventh president* said he was through with politics in his famous "Checkers" speech.

b. The judge said, "You *the defendant* are a menace to society."

c. His home run *what a blast!* made it over the center field fence in record time.

d. The monetary part of the reward *$50* wasn't nearly as important as the recognition.

e. In her last speech to Torvald, Nora declares her independence: "I'm freeing you from being *responsible There* has to be absolute freedom for us both" *64.* [The original direct quotation, from page 64 of Ibsen's *A Doll's House,* is as follows: "I'm freeing you from being responsible. Don't feel yourself bound, any more than I will. There has to be absolute freedom for us both."]

1. Mark went to his first FFA *Future Farmers of America* meetings when he was only ten.

2. Walt Whitman mourns the death of Abraham Lincoln in the poem beginning with these famous lines: "O Captain! my Captain! our fearful trip is *done, The* ship has weather'd every rack, the prize we sought is won." [The lines from the poem read:

    O Captain! my Captain! our fearful trip is done,

    The ship has weather'd every rack, the prize we sought is won.]

3. While in the Boston area, we visited four historical *places North* Bridge, Lexington Green, Paul Revere's House, and Old North *Church related* to the start of the Revolution.

4. June 18 is the birthday of two highly creative people*: me b. 1950 and Paul McCartney b. 1942.*

5. If there's any advantage to having to eat in the dormitory, it's that I don't have to eat food I don't *like liver,* broccoli, tuna casserole.

52–1   UNDERLINING (ITALICS)

Underline words and terms as necessary in the following sentences. Change any underlining that is not correct. (You may have to add quotation marks in some sentences.) If you need help with this exercise, see Section 52 in *Keys for Writers: A Brief Handbook.*

Example: The <u>New York Times</u> is among America's most respected news

sources, but I also rely on my local <u>Riverton Gazette</u>.

   a. The French use the term bon appetit at the beginning of a meal; many

Americans now say simply, "Enjoy."

   b. The poem <u>Song of Myself</u> appears in Walt Whitman's collection <u>Leaves

of Grass</u>.

   c. My two-year-old uses the word dog to refer to any animal.

   d. Most Americans know the Latin word for tree, which is arbor.

   e. I've seen the movie Cinema Paradiso four times, and I intend to see it at

least four more.

   1. Do you take the creation story in <u>Genesis</u> literally?

   2. That sunset was the most <u>amazing</u> sight I have ever seen.

   3. The film The Dead is based on James Joyce's short story The Dead.

   4. The song <u>Sunshine of Your Love</u> is from the album "Disraeli Gears" by

the group <u>Cream</u>.

   5. The word hellion <u>certainly</u> applies to my adolescent niece.

53–1 CAPITALIZATION

Edit the following sentences for correct use of capital letters. If a sentence is correct, write "correct" after it. If you need help with this exercise, see Section 53 in *Keys for Writers: A Brief Handbook.*

Example: In ~~High~~ ~~School~~, I was editor of the newspaper *The Cardinal.*

(handwritten correction: high school)

a. The mayor of New Market, Johanna Hindeman, attended the Memorial Day fireworks every year.

b. The republican party was known as the antislavery party at the time of the civil war.

c. During Fall Semester our Architecture class visited Rockefeller center, the Empire State building, and St. Patrick's cathedral.

d. Mahatma Gandhi applied the principles of Civil Disobedience to his struggle for Indian independence.

e. Virginia Cusack, Executive Vice President, was known to most of the workers as Ginny.

1. F. Scott Fitzgerald's short story "The diamond as big as the Ritz" contains a theme that would reappear in *The great Gatsby.*

2. Whether you head east to east Orange, south to south Carolina, or north to north Dakota, you're sure to find a McDonald's.

3. When did Patrick Henry say, "give me liberty or give me death"?

4. We made a left onto Chestnut street instead of a right and ended up on Ramada boulevard.

5. The norman conquest of England, led by William the conqueror, started in 1066.

54–1 ABBREVIATIONS

Edit the following sentences for correct use of abbreviations. If a sentence is correct, write "correct" after it. If you need help with this exercise, see Section 54 in *Keys for Writers: A Brief Handbook.*

Example: Try to get that ~~info(~~ information to me by ~~Tues. a.m.(~~ Tuesday morning.

a. Doctor Ruth Mullen was my pediatrician, and now she is my children's.

b. The students wondered how they would get through all of chap. 5 in one night.

c. My older brother still does not know how to program his VCR.

d. The men voted to stay overnight in NYC, but the women voted to continue on to Phila.

e. The F.B.I., the C.I.A., and the I.R.S. don't have the best reputations with the Amer. public.

1. We measured the plot in meters, not in yds.

2. Jordan Reynolds has two M.A.'s and one Ph.D.

3. My brother-in-law said he was bringing everyone he could think of—his mother, father, sisters, brothers, aunts, etc.—to my family's reunion.

4. My superstitious sister's birthday, Oct. 13, will fall on a Fri. this year.

5. The dimensions of carry-on luggage cannot exceed 41 in. (105 cm) in length, height, and width added together.

55–1 NUMBERS

Edit the following sentences for correct use of numbers (assume the conventions of the humanities). If a sentence is correct, write "correct" after it. If you need help with this exercise, see Section 55 in *Keys for Writers: A Brief Handbook*.

Example: Of the eleven people at the party, ~~7~~ *seven* were old friends, ~~2~~ *two* were colleagues, and ~~2~~ *two* were relatives.

a. On seven December 1941, Japanese planes attacked Pearl Harbor.

b. We counted twenty-seven sailboats on the lake yesterday afternoon.

c. To get ready for the race, Yvonne ran 3 miles one day, 5 miles the next, and 8 miles the next.

d. Nell took exactly one dollar and twenty-seven cents from her piggy bank when she went to the candy store.

e. 12 times this year I've asked my neighbors to keep their dog tied up during the day when they're at work.

1. Ms. Brimley has lived at twenty-five Grand Boulevard all her life.

2. After three periods the hockey playoff game was tied seven to seven and the teams were headed into overtime.

3. We drove 1/2 mile beyond the end of the paved road before deciding that we were lost and should turn around.

4. The average grade on the calculus test was sixty-two before the professor applied the curve.

5. I took 3 semesters of Spanish, and I think I need 3 more before I will feel comfortable traveling on my own in South America.

56–1 HYPHENATION

Add or delete hyphens as necessary in the following sentences. If a sentence is correct, write "correct" after it. If you need help with this exercise, see Section 56 in *Keys for Writers: A Brief Handbook*.

Example: He did a first-rate job on that budget movie.

a. After the accident, Jake was semi-conscious, and it took him forty five minutes to remember his own name.

b. Three quarters of the way through the test, I realized I didn't remember enough about post Reconstruction America to answer the last essay question.

c. The short term profit was a relief to the fledgling CEO.

d. Her way out ideas have led to some really-innovative advances in medical treatment.

e. The half price items at the yard sale included a gas powered leaf blower.

1. It was a store for do it yourself homeowners. Walter, the fix it man, loved it.

2. The lost hiker was well bundled against the elements, but he was half starved and frightened.

3. In a public spirited gesture, the owners of the automobile dealership gave the homeless shelter the use of a van every night.

4. Because the all important high ratings failed to materialize, the network decided to cancel the usually-entertaining sitcom.

5. More and more anti-wrinkle creams are being sold over the counter.

58–1 SPELLING

Correct any spelling errors in the following sentences. If a sentence is correct, write "correct" after it. If you need help with this exercise, see Section 58 in *Keys for Writers: A Brief Handbook.*

Example: She was an old acquaintᵉnce, but I'm not sure I would describe her as a friᵉᵉnd.

a. Gertrude was very embarassed when her pocketbook spilled open on the subway train.

b. Most young people want independance from their parents, but many of them also want thier parents to continue to support them, if only emotionaly.

c. In the beginning, my writing contained a lot of awkward phrases.

d. My sociology professor is very knowledgable, but sometimes her knowledge interfers with common sense.

e. Our seventh-grade teacher always told us that our grammer was good but that we mispelled too much.

1. Sometimes it takes the band members half a day to set up their equiptment.

2. Do you know whether he is celebrating his thirty-eigth or fourtieth birthday?

3. The young violinist who just won a position with the orchestra now has to decide whether to persue her college education first.

4. As soon as Louis gets his licence, he will be able to drive us anywhere we want to go in his father's convertable.

5. She publicly announced her candidacy for attorney general.

58–2 SPELLING

On the line next to each of the following words, write the correct spelling if the word is spelled incorrectly. If the word is correct, write "correct" after it. If you need help with this exercise, see Section 58 in *Keys for Writers: A Brief Handbook.*

Example: churchs (plural) ___churches___

a. leafs (plural) _____

b. percieve _____

c. offerred _____

d. economies (plural) _____

e. prettyest _____

1. criteria (plural) _____

2. writting _____

_____

3. radioes (plural) _____

4. publicly _____

_____

5. parodys (plural) _____

6. tieing _____

7. monkies (plural)

8. seize _____

9. tooths (plural)

10. accidently _____

PART 9
FOR MULTILINGUAL/ESL
WRITERS

60–1 CATEGORIES OF NOUNS AND NOUN PLURALS

Identify the nouns in the following sentences as either proper nouns (P), countable common nouns (CC), or uncountable common nouns (UC), and correct any incorrect verbs or adjectives. If you need help with this exercise, see Sections 60a, b in *Keys for Writers: A Brief Handbook.*

Example:
             CC   P   CC
  Thousands of tourists visits the Sphinx each year.

    a. Westminster Abbey is one of the oldest churches in England.

    b. Many people believes they have been abducted by aliens from space.

    c. Times Square has experienced a renaissance in recent years.

    d. The *New York Times* employs many excellents reporters.

    e. Jell-O is a brand of gelatin frequently used in making low-fats desserts.

    1. All three brothers works for the Army Corps of Engineers.

    2. Sue and Mike like to talk on the telephone about music, art, and literature.

    3. The accountant asked his clients for more information about their delinquents accounts.

    4. June's favorites pastimes includes sports, music, and cooking.

    5. Leo visited the Eiffel Tower in June with his goods friends Rick and Mary.

60–2 NOUNS AND ARTICLES   *22 pts back page*

Edit the following sentences, adding or changing articles as needed and deleting any articles that are not needed. If you need help with this exercise, see Section 60 in *Keys for Writers: A Brief Handbook.*   *Each sentence has 1 – 3 errors.*

Example: **On my first, one-day visit to ~~the~~ Washington, D.C., I wasn't**

sure which sights to see first.

a. The line of tourists at a White House was already quite long, winding

along a street next to the White House lawn toward the Ellipse.

b. I walked around an Ellipse and up small hill to a Washington

Monument.

c. A line there was not as long, so I waited underneath the circle of fifty

flags, a one for every state in the United States.

d. From an information in my guidebook, I learned that the monument is

555 feet tall and was a tallest structure in world when it was built in

1886.

e. From observation area at a top of a monument I could see all of

Washington spread out before me.

1. Across the Mall I could see a Capitol Building and the other museums

lining the Mall.

2. Toward a west I could see the monument to the President Lincoln,

toward an east the monument to President Jefferson.

3. Beyond those two monuments was a meandering Potomac River.

4. Not until I came down from the top of the monument and began

   walking across Mall did I realize that a scale of all buildings masks

   distances between them.

5. I also realized that I would be doing great deal of a walking in a city

   before a day had ended.

60–3 NOUNS AND ARTICLES

Edit the following sentences for correct use of articles. You may need to add and delete articles, change the form of some nouns, and add other words. If a sentence is correct, write "correct" after it. If you need help with this exercise, see Section 60 in *Keys for Writers: A Brief Handbook.*

Example: We drove to ~~a~~ Delaware Water Gap to look at ~~a~~ scenery.
(the inserted before Delaware and before scenery)

a. I put a potato in the oven and then went out to the store. Hour later I had to phone my sister and ask her to take a potato out of the oven.

b. The money can't buy a happiness, but it can pay a grocery bill.

c. Which country in the South America is your roommate from?

d. Jorge asked his mother for an advice about living away from a home for a first time.

e. She ordered a hamburger and fries. Fries were delivered first; by the time a hamburger arrived at her table, she had finished eating all the fries.

1. We went for a walk under stars. After the hour, it got very cold and a walk became a run.

2. When my parents set up a bakery in small storefront, they had to buy several equipments such as the oven and the huge freezer.

3. Mario was a tallest boy in a sixth-grade class.

4. A neighbor who works the night shift asked me to feed his cat before I go to bed.

5. I poured a cereal into a bowl on the counter and then added a milk.

6. The Fondinis visit their family in Italy in the June and July every year.

7. Willie turned off his alarm clock and turned on a TV across from his bed to find out what a weather was going to be today.

8. The honesty is a best policy.

9. We had been planning a picnic for the months. When the day of a picnic finally arrived, we remembered a bottle of wine we'd bought for the occasion but forgot a corkscrew to open a bottle.

10. In our culture class, we're reading a French, Spanish, and African literature.

61–1   THE *BE* AUXILIARY

Edit the following sentences for correct use of the *be* auxiliary and the correct form of the following verb. If a sentence is correct, write "correct" after it. If you need help with this exercise, see Section 61a in *Keys for Writers: A Brief Handbook.*

Example: She has ~~dance~~ since the party began.

been dancing

a.   They eat now.

b.   The pool be drained last month.

c.   The skyscraper build in only three months.

d.   She was still looking for her glasses when the movie began.

e.   June dieting for six weeks.

1.   The plane take off when the rain began.

2.   Marcia sing in tonight's concert.

3.   The cook was toss the salad when the rolls burned.

4.   The company was losing money on its new product line.

5.   That sweater made in Scotland.

61–2 MODAL AUXILIARY VERBS

In each of the following sentences, use the correct form of the verb in brackets, preceded by an appropriate modal auxiliary verb or verbs. Use the meaning suggested in brackets as a guide. If you need help with this exercise, see Section 61b in *Keys for Writers: A Brief Handbook*.

Example: He __will clean__ his room tomorrow. [*clean;* intention]

a. If the baby does not sleep too much during the day, she _____

   well tonight. [*sleep;* expectation]

b. My mother is standing on my front doorstep. I _____ the

   door when I went out. [*lock;* logical assumption]

c. If we had known you were coming, we _____ set an extra

   place at the table. [*set;* speculation]

d. I _____ the floor before my company arrives. [*wash;*

   necessity]

e. I _____ not _____ a visa because I applied too

   late. [*get;* ability]

1. She said we _____ away during spring break. [*go;* possibility]

2. He _____ calculus before he entered high school. [*understand;*

   ability]

3. When we went to the beach every summer, we _____ huge

   sand castles every day. [*build;* repeated action]

4. `She's not on this plane; she _____ on the next one. [*be;*

   possibility or logical assumption]

5. We _____ fertilizing the lawn before it rains. [*finish;*

   necessity]

6. If you want to finish college in three years, you _____ your

   course schedule more carefully. [*plan;* advisability]

7. We _____ to the movies if we aren't too tired. [*go;* intention]

8. If I had written to you sooner, you _____ my plans. [*know;*

   speculation]

9. We told them our plans; they _____ we wouldn't be here until

   this afternoon. [*know;* expectation]

10. We _____ our plane tickets by now. [*receive;* expectation]

61–3   VERBS FOLLOWED BY AN INFINITIVE OR *-ING* VERBAL

Edit the following sentences, using the correct verbal forms. If a sentence is correct, write "correct" after it. If you need help with this exercise, see Sections 61c–e in *Keys for Writers: A Brief Handbook.*

Example: Claudia did not expect ~~failing~~ to fail her exam because she had studied

hard.

a. The principal ordered the tardy student staying after school every day

for a week.

b. The committee discussed adopting the proposal but postponed to vote

on it until the next meeting.

c. On her first trip to Hawaii, she could not imagine to be in a more

beautiful place on earth.

d. Tony persuaded his mother allowing him to take the family car

overnight.

e. We can no longer pretend being uninvolved.

1. The counselor told me to try to remember as much as possible about my

childhood.

2. The bossy older sister enjoyed to make her timid younger sister clear

the table after every meal.

3. My parents always encouraged me to be independent and honest.

4. Jackson disliked to take the baby to the doctor.

5. Madeleine finished to study after her friends left.

6. Don't delay to send in your money for the tickets.

7. All her adult life my grandmother has avoided to eat raisins because she was forced to eat them during the Depression.

8. I will not deny to run the red light, but I hope no one asks.

9. Did the clerk suggest to give you a rain check for the chair that was on sale?

10. The sign warned visitors swimming at their own risk.

61–4 VERBALS USED AS ADJECTIVES

Edit the following sentences, using the correct form of verbals used as adjectives. If a sentence is correct, write "correct" after it. If you need help with this exercise, see Section 61f in *Keys for Writers: A Brief Handbook*.

Example: The ~~excited~~ ^exciting^ finish to the ballgame made us all go home feeling exhilarated. ~~exhilarating.~~

a. I am always annoying by my little brother's early morning noise when I am trying to sleep late.

b. The statistics on underage drinking and driving are very depressed.

c. Sarah reluctantly brought her disappointed first-semester report card home to her parents.

d. The worried director made her exhausting cast run through the play one more time.

e. We couldn't imagine a more bored lecture, but we kept ourselves amusing by passing notes across the back row.

1. One of my most embarrassed moments was setting off the bakery's alarm one morning before it was open.

2. The surprising look on their faces told us that our little secret had worked.

3. Toby's grandfather spun a fascinated tale of life in the coal mines.

4. Tonight's algebra homework consists of the most confused problems I've ever seen.

5. The stunning family received the shocked news without comment.

62–1 SENTENCE STRUCTURE

Edit the following sentences, making sure that sentence elements are complete and in the correct order. If a sentence is correct, write "correct" after it. If you need help with this exercise, see Sections 62a–c in *Keys for Writers: A Brief Handbook.*

Example: Steve bought [for his little brother] a hot dog| at the baseball

   game.

   a. The committee sent to the alleged witness a subpoena.

   b. Professor Moran explained the class exponential functions.

   c. I have to find my mother a gift for her birthday.

   d. The meteorology students visited yesterday Mount Washington.

   e. Bob ran every morning because helped him keep in shape.

   1. The library's director opened us the room containing the rare books.

   2. Her roommate offered her the rugs they had bought at the beginning of

       the year.

   3. The Tigers and White Sox broke last season the record for most home

       runs in a nine-inning game.

   4. He sold the reconditioned GTO his best friend.

   5. Are two reasons why he to the store returned the shoes.

62–2 DIRECT AND INDIRECT QUOTATIONS AND QUESTIONS

Rewrite each of the following direct quotations or questions as an indirect quotation or question, making appropriate changes in subjects and verb forms. If you need help with this exercise, see Section 62d in *Keys for Writers: A Brief Handbook*.

Example: Professor Alfonso told her students, ~~"Do your~~ to do their homework in blue books tonight."

a. During the inquiry, he kept repeating, "I didn't see a thing."

b. "Plant these impatiens in a shady corner of the flowerbed," the woman at the garden shop told us.

c. She asked, "Do you want to taste the brownies?" I said, "Sure, I want to taste them."

d. My cousin asked, "Do you remember the summer we spent on Granddad's farm?"

e. As she stepped out of the car at the airport terminal, Carla told her father, "Please don't bother, I can handle my bags myself."

1. "Why did you sit in traffic instead of taking the back roads?" we asked when they arrived two hours late.

2. "Are we going to the zoo or the aquarium first?" the little girl asked her father.

3. "I've never been able to do twenty push-ups at a time," she said.

4. "Don't come unprepared to the exam," the teacher said.

5. He asked, "Where are they going?"

63–1 IDIOMATIC STRUCTURES

Edit the following sentences, adding, deleting, or changing prepositions as necessary for correct use with adjectives and verbs. If a sentence is correct, write "correct" after it. If you need help with this exercise, see Section 63 in *Keys for Writers: A Brief Handbook*.

Example: Are you aware ^of the rules for claiming the prize?

a. The dissatisfied passenger wrote a letter complaining for the lack of food on the four-hour train trip.

b. She has always been interested at archaeology.

c. When we arrived at Florence, we weren't sure whether to go to the Duomo or the Uffizi first.

d. He was content by his low-paying entry-level job because it left him time for his real passion: scuba diving.

e. We can't blame our parents on everything that happens to us in life.

1. After their luggage was stolen, they had to rely to the sun to wake them up in the morning.

2. I have never been fond to tulips: they are too tall and spindly.

3. The troop leader worried for her girls' safety every minute they were hiking through the woods.

4. The lecture was supposed to be held at the seminar room but was moved to the auditorium to accommodate the crowd at the door.

5. The children were tired at the endless bickering of their parents.

6. Even though I was intensely jealous by his success, I made myself congratulate him being made a partner in the firm.

7. The detective was suspicious of every move the suspect made after eight o'clock the night of the robbery.

8. Will social security still be available to take care for our needs when we retire?

9. He was never sorry at any unkind words he said.

10. The students found it very hard to concentrate their studies after the fire alarm went off for the third time.

63–2 IDIOMATIC STRUCTURES

Edit the following sentences, making sure that idiomatic expressions with verbs and verbals are used correctly. If a sentence is correct, write "correct" after it. If you need help with this exercise, see Section 63 in *Keys for Writers: A Brief Handbook*.

Example: The owners and the players held talks for three days. They

broke ~~off them~~ when they couldn't agree on any of the issues

on the table.

a. My cousin told me to look up him if I was ever in Idaho.

b. Do you think she takes after her mother or her father?

c. The team members counted to the high-scoring forward to make up for their shaky defense.

d. Whenever she lists the seven capital sins, she leaves sloth.

e. The students were looking forward to travel to Washington during spring break.

1. The test was canceled because of the snowstorm, so we have to make up it next Saturday.

2. Before the surgeon general's warnings, many pregnant women used to drink alcohol without thinking about it.

3. Looking at the crowd lined at the front door, the soup kitchen volunteers were afraid they might run out bread.

4. If you're unsure of an answer, leave out it and go back if you have time at the end.

5. My younger sister always got away things I was punished for.

6. In the textile mills young girls worked for more than eight hours without to take a break.

7. When we moved to the Northeast we had to get used to shovel snow and scrape ice off our cars every morning.

8. The journalist ended up in jail because he stood up to what he thought was right.

9. What kinds of role models do young people look up today?

10. After three attacks in the campus parking lot, the university police decided to look in adding extra patrols.

ANSWERS TO LETTERED EXERCISES

29–1 REPETITION AND REDUNDANCY, page 1

Suggested revisions:

a. Harold thought that if he submitted his resignation the group would fall apart.
b. Every candidate for the scholarship must provide two letters of reference.
c. From the airplane we could see coral reefs in the blue-green Caribbean.
d. We were hoping to find a motel with a decent restaurant and a laundry.
e. Parkinson's Law states that work expands to fill the time available for its completion.

30–1 ACTION VERBS, page 3

Suggested revisions:

a. Thirteen children have signed up to go to the Museum of Science.
b. She wrote a letter complaining about the poor service at the post office.
c. We preferred taking an early flight.
d. I have only one more thing to do before I leave for Seattle.
e. Maurice will not make it to the major leagues this year.

33–1 APPROPRIATE LANGUAGE, page 4

Suggested revisions:

a. I went to the car dealer to buy a new car.
b. Taking advantage of a chance to make a profit, the board of directors voted to sell the radio station.
c. My boss rejected my idea, saying it was not workable.
d. While staying in Beverly Hills, they took a walk in the neighborhood where movie stars live.
e. Lack of rainfall and very high temperatures threaten the corn crop.

33–2   APPROPRIATE LANGUAGE, page 5

Suggested revisions:

a. With tires screaming, the police car sped off after the robbers.
b. The supervisor met with each department head before the sales conference.
c. The novel is definitely a masterpiece.
d. I asked my parents for the car but my sister had already asked them.
e. Our captain tried to motivate us for the big game.

33–3   APPROPRIATE LANGUAGE, page 6

Suggested revisions:

a. Each supervisor was warned that the workers might strike without notice.
b. All the congressional representatives on the committee voted to send the bill to the full House.
c. The new clinic helps patients with breast cancer.
d. The Girl Scouts staffed the table in front of the grocery store to sell cookies.
e. Off-duty police officers sometimes encounter crimes in progress.

34–1   NOUNS, page 7

a. election, chairperson, commission, times
b. Ben Franklin, name, Poor Richard, almanac
c. chickens, pen
d. building's, owner, buyers
e. Ticks, time, skin

34–2   PRONOUNS, page 8

Suggested answers:

a. Myrna is a dancer who knows when she is performing well.
b. Everyone is welcome at any time.
c. My brother and sister arrived unexpectedly. I haven't seen them in more than a year.

    d. This book is mine; that one is yours.

    e. Even Roberto himself could not find his own house.

34–3 VERBS, page 9

    a. V: praised

    b. V: know; LV: is; AUX: Do

    c. LV: is, is

    d. V: ran

    e. V: know, disappeared, telling; AUX: am

34–4 ADJECTIVES, page 10

Suggested answers:

    a. The had to prepare two bedrooms because their sprightly aunt and elderly grandmother were coming to visit.

    b. My stubborn dog has been very disobedient since I took her to obedience school.

    c. Our paper was supposed to be on a Dickens novel.

    d. After a late night of partying, we were not very energetic at the next morning's classes.

    e. They had to wade through shallow water to reach the dilapidated boat tied to the white dock.

34–5 ADVERBS, page 12

Suggested answers:

    a. I had to hire someone to organize my files efficiently.

    b. The painting was a quite remarkable achievement.

    c. The swallows return faithfully to Capistrano every March.

    d. He was running out of time, so he had to write hastily in his blue book.

    e. The concert attracted nearly one hundred thousand people on a somewhat chilly June night.

34–6 PREPOSITIONS, page 13

Suggested answers:

a. The soldiers returned home weary after the war.
b. We looked over the edge at the green valley below.
c. I've never known true peace until now.
d. Through the long night the mother sat by her baby's side.
e. Between the bridges flowed a teeming river.

34–7 CONJUNCTIONS, page 14

Suggested answers:

a. Vera had looked forward to reading the new novel, so she was disappointed that it was so boring. (coordinating conjunction) *Or* Vera had looked forward to reading the new novel; therefore, she was disappointed that it was so boring. (conjunctive adverb)
b. Mark crept quietly toward the deer and the fawn because he wanted to take pictures of them. (subordinating conjunction)
c. She tried to sleep whenever the sound of sirens diminished. (subordinating conjunction)
d. We can't bring any food to camp; moreover, we will receive mail only twice a week. (conjunctive adverb)
e. As visitors lined up outside the museum entrance, officials tried to decide whether to open the doors early. (subordinating conjunction)

34–8 SENTENCE PATTERNS, page 16

a. Subject: Ernest Hemingway; verb: was; subject complement: an ambulance driver in France
b. Subject: We; verb: gave; indirect object: our plants; direct object: a good dose of water
c. Subject: The book club; verb: offered; indirect object: new members; direct objects: a tote bag and four free books
d. Subject: The thunder and lightning; verb: made; direct object: the children; object complement: fearful
e. Subject: the party; verb: seemed; subject complement: tame

34–9 PHRASES, page 17

Suggested revisions:

a. At the start of their vacation, they were unhappy about the price of gasoline.
b. Encountering no opposition, the troops plunged into the wild jungle.
c. He is a seasoned politician, and to say what he means takes real effort.
d. The breeze having died down, we motored to shore.
e. Stunned by her defeat, the incumbent governor vowed to run again.

34–10 CLAUSES: COORDINATION, page 19

Suggested revisions:

a. More people should learn how to use computers, for they will play an ever larger part in our future.
b. Marco hasn't turned in a single paper this semester; in fact, he hasn't turned in a piece of homework.
c. We could play at the park tomorrow if it doesn't rain, or we could play at the Y if it does.
d. John F. Kennedy was president for less than three years, yet he was one of our most admired presidents.
e. Samantha's grades were better this semester than last; moreover, she was happier.

34–11 CLAUSES: SUBORDINATION, page 21

Suggested revisions:

a. After every heavy downpour, I have to run two electric fans in my cellar because the floor and walls are damp.
b. The woolly mammoth, which is an extinct species of elephant, once roamed the northern parts of Europe, Asia, and North America.
c. The children tracked mud across the freshly washed floor as they came in from playing in the rain.
d. Local farmers who grow corn, peppers, and tomatoes sell their produce at roadside stands starting around Memorial Day.
e. Whoever was lurking in the shadows was taken to the police station for questioning.

35-1 SENTENCE TYPES, page 25

a. Compound
b. Complex; dependent clauses: Whereas an ophthalmologist is a medical doctor, who specializes in the eyes
c. Compound-complex; dependent clause: Unless you tell us otherwise
d. Simple
e. Compound

36-1 PARALLELISM, page 27

Suggested revisions:

a. To be comfortable at the campsite, they not only wanted to light a decent fire for cooking but also needed to have access to an electrical hookup.
b. Tom liked bowling on Saturday afternoons and fishing with his neighbor.
c. Listening to the crickets chirp in the country is better than being bombarded by traffic noise in the city.
d. Dinah could throw a boomerang with accuracy, clean a trout in under a minute, and paddle a canoe expertly.
e. Betsy was overjoyed and excited when she heard the news.

38-1 SENTENCE FRAGMENTS, page 29

Suggested revisions:

a. I'll be happy to help you if I have the time.
b. Since 1979, because of a proposal made by the United States, the World Meteorological Organization has given hurricanes male and female names.
c. Correct
d. I doubt that the author was referring to the Native Americans, since Western civilization has made it nearly impossible for them to participate in "the system."
e. In my culture, which feels that women are not as important as men, it is a constant struggle for a woman to gain the respect of a man.

38–2 SENTENCE FRAGMENTS, page 31

Suggested revisions:

a. My husband and I are always running out of money by the end of the month.
b. Knowing that Fred would be there, I hurried home to see my long-lost cousin.
c. The Vietnam Memorial, near the Lincoln Memorial, was dedicated on November 13, 1982.
d. My brother couldn't decide whether to name his first baby Edison or Harrison—after the inventor or the actor.
e. The lawn needs fertilizer and seed in the spring, and it needs mowing and watering in the summer.

39–1 RUN-ONS AND COMMA SPLICES, page 33

Suggested revisions:

a. Some people love celebrating their birthdays, but some people would just as soon forget them.
b. I know someone who has credit cards and likes to spend money.
c. My mother always said, "Don't run down the stairs." She was right.
d. When we were children, our parents let us sell lemonade in front of our house; times have changed, however.
e. He's not working now; he's still at home.

39–2 RUN-ONS AND COMMA SPLICES, page 35

Suggested revisions:

a. The so-called marriage tax means that married people sometimes pay more than they would if they were just living together. That doesn't make sense.
b. Correct
c. Sharon dedicated her life to Paul; in return he dedicated his life to his job.
d. Last month our middle school sponsored a "TV turnoff," the purpose of which was to show children that they can have fun without watching television.
e. You need to plan now; otherwise your retirement income will be too little for you to live on.

40–1 SENTENCE SNARLS: DANGLING AND MISPLACED MODIFIERS, page 37

Suggested revisions:

a. She asked whether the butcher shop that we frequently patronize has fresh turkey.
b. Visitors can journey back to a town that, nestled between two mountains, has remained unchanged for two centuries.
c. By the day after Christmas, the children had broken almost all their toys.
d. Sensing that the students weren't prepared, Mr. Sanchez postponed the pop quiz.
e. Having finished nearly all the pie, we wrapped the rest in plastic wrap.

40–2 SENTENCE SNARLS: DANGLING AND MISPLACED MODIFIERS, page 39

Suggested revisions:

a. The archaeologists found almost an entire dinosaur skeleton.
b. Because the automobile insurance cost more than we expected, we could afford only the legal minimum amount.
c. The job that she thought would completely hold her interest bored her. *Or* The job that she thought would hold her interest bored her completely.
d. Eager to see Fort Sumter, we took the tour boat across Charleston Harbor.
e. The picnic table and benches that we just finished painting are on the lawn.

40–3 SENTENCE SNARLS: SHIFTS, MIXED CONSTRUCTIONS, DEFINITIONS, AND REASONS, page 41

Suggested revisions:

a. Agent Orange defoliated millions of acres of Vietnamese countryside and caused health problems to many Vietnam veterans.
b. Our professor told us to pick up our blue books before we sat down but not to start writing until she gave us final instructions.

c. The reason the heat came on is that the temperature outside dropped below fifty degrees. *Or* The heat came on because the temperature outside dropped below fifty degrees.

d. The IRS agent demanded that Maureen bring all her receipts for the past year as well as her daily calendar and her checkbook.

e. To do a handspring full twist, the gymnast pushes off the floor with both hands, snaps her feet around over her head, pushes off with her feet, and does a 360-degree twist in the air before landing.

40–4 SENTENCE SNARLS: FAULTY PREDICATION, page 43

Suggested revisions:

a. Climbing the last thousand feet of the Mauna Kea volcano made us dizzy and lightheaded.

b. As an African American student who went to a high school in Brooklyn that had a student body seventy percent white, I sometimes could not face one more day in school.

c. Rita's attempt to appear polite and gracious backfired and made her appear rude and ungrateful.

d. Her weightlifting over the winter has improved Mary Jane's effectiveness as a power pitcher.

e. For all your absences this semester, your grade will drop by half a point.

40–5 SENTENCE SNARLS: ADVERB CLAUSE AS SUBJECT, OMITTED WORDS, RESTATED SUBJECT, page 45

Suggested revisions:

a. Noriaki's depression contributes to his family's concern.

b. My aunt and uncle can live and have lived for years without leaving the island.

c. All the neighbors wondered how the two boys could possibly get away with such a blatant crime.

d. The hothouse tomatoes from the farmstand are as expensive as but tastier than those from the gourmet market.

e. The child who wandered into the aisle during the service was quickly snatched up by her mother.

41–1 REGULAR AND IRREGULAR VERB FORMS, AUXILIARIES, MODALS, page 47

Suggested revisions:

a. We had driven fifteen miles before Mark told us about the money he had lost gambling last week.
b. Correct
c. She had gone with him five times before her parents found out.
d. She set the keys on the table with such a crash that it woke the cat.
e. I might not win the contest, but I have made a good attempt.

41–2 VERB TENSES, page 49

Suggested revisions:

a. ran
b. will be doing
c. is
d. embodies
e. had worked, postponed

41–3 VERB TENSES, page 51

Suggested revisions:

a. They will not take a vote until all the committee members are seated.
b. Some people look away when they see an accident, but I like to study such things.
c. They owned the business for twenty-five years.
d. Battles used to be fought with swords and maces, which were used to crush armor.
e. The football coach got so upset by the call that he stuck his head in the water bucket.

41–4 VERBS: *-ED* ENDINGS, page 53

Suggested revisions:

a. The new edition of the textbook has corrected the errors in the first edition.
b. Because she had had four years of Italian in high school, she was able to skip to the advanced course in freshman year of college.
c. After eight hours, he had accomplished his goal of sanding the entire face of the house.
d. The school committee decided to postpone a vote on the proposed renovations to the middle school.
e. Once the conversation turned to adult matters, Celia excused herself from the table and went to her room.

41–5 VERBS IN CONDITIONAL SENTENCES AND IN WISHES, REQUESTS, AND DEMANDS, page 55

Suggested revisions:

a. When the temperature drops below thirty-two degrees, water freezes.
b. If the workers voted today, they would not be able to agree on a settlement with management.
c. She would have known that the butler was innocent if she had kept careful notes and had paid attention to the witnesses.
d. If he were sixty-two, he would retire without a second thought.
e. The principal demanded that we bring a note from our parents about our absence.

42–1 PASSIVE VOICE, page 57

Suggested revisions:

a. The bombs were dropped by a B-52 bomber, and the damage was spotted by a spy plane.
b. The blood samples are being analyzed for their DNA content.
c. Correct
d. The audience was stumped by the magician; a girl in the audience was even turned into a crow.
e. Oval Office conversations were taped by Richard Nixon.

43–1 AGREEMENT, page 59

a. knows
b. leads
c. talk
d. are
e. has

43–2 AGREEMENT, page 61

a. There were an otter and three whales at Point Lobos yesterday.
b. Her grades are the only thing that matters to her parents.
c. The home unit of the soldiers who were lost last week is throwing them a party.
d. At the start of the movie, from the depths of the seas emerges a magnificent whale.
e. Do the butter and the sugar go into the bowl before the flour?

43–3 AGREEMENT, page 63

a. Correct
b. Recycling or bringing trash to local dumps is recommended for trash removal.
c. Either the sculpture or the paintings are intended for the foyer.
d. For several seconds after the curtain came down, there was neither clapping nor cheering.
e. Several cookies in the last batch were burned.

43–4 AGREEMENT, page 64

a. Correct
b. Either of her teachers was willing to give her credit for effort.
c. A great deal of pain and suffering was a natural by-product of the explosion.
d. The team wasn't ready to play, and it showed.
e. The wrappings from a hasty lunch were left on the desk.

44–1 PRONOUN FORMS, page 65

a. Is it okay for you and me to go to the play today?
b. Our lockers are clean; theirs are a mess.
c. Albert thinks that no one can jump better than he.
d. Correct
e. He didn't like my singing along with the record.

44–2 PRONOUN REFERENCE, page 67

Suggested revisions:

a. I got a letter from the bank about a bounced check, but no one answered the phone when I called to explain.
b. In his work, Tim O'Brien recounts in many different forms his experiences in Vietnam.
c. After an adventurous first lesson, José told Manuel that Manuel would never learn to drive. *Or* After an adventurous first lesson, José told Manuel, "I will never learn to drive."
d. The newspaper article says that children today spend more time watching TV than their parents did.
e. I planted a bush in the garden next to the house; now I just have to remember to water the garden every day.

44–3 PRONOUN AGREEMENT, page 69

Suggested revisions:

a. All students should know their locker numbers.
b. In its year-end report, the company gave its stockholders the bad news.
c. Every job applicant is required to state whether he or she has been convicted of any crimes in the past five years. *Or* All job applicants are required to state whether they have been convicted of any crimes in the past five years.
d. Everyone on the boys' soccer team is responsible for keeping his own uniform clean.
e. Correct

44–4 FORMS OF THE PRONOUN *WHO*, page 71

a. Give this book to whoever wants it.
b. I asked the manager who was in charge of customer service.
c. Correct
d. Whom should we ask to play the piano, her or Lupè?
e. She wrote an article about whom the coach intended to use in the next game.

45–1 ADJECTIVES AND ADVERBS, page 72

a. If you don't do well on the test, you may have to repeat the course.
b. He acted so unreasonably that we had to leave the party early.
c. She darted quickly between the opposing players and then dribbled swiftly for the basket.
d. They could scarcely contain their excitement on arriving in Rome.
e. The moon did not appear very bright even though it was full tonight.

45–2 PLACEMENT OF ADJECTIVES AND ADVERBS, page 74

a. When we pulled into the lot we saw many expensive red cars, but we were looking for an inexpensive white car.
b. The buttons were sewn perfectly onto the sweater.
c. To cheer me up on this dreary day, I brought along my huge new flowered umbrella.
d. The rain fell steadily throughout the day.
e. The nondescript, abandoned green building on the corner is being turned into a little gray Catholic church.

45–3 COMPARATIVE AND SUPERLATIVE FORMS OF ADJECTIVES AND ADVERBS, page 75

Suggested revisions:

a. He claimed that his expensive new shoes helped him to run more quickly than he'd ever run before.
b. The larger of my feet is a full half-inch longer than the smaller.
c. Henry's painting is good, but Amy's is even better.
d. No one could feel worse than I feel today.

e. My sister and I were always competitive, but we reached a silent agreement: she was prettier but I was smarter.

45–4 FAULTY OR INCOMPLETE COMPARISONS, page 77

Suggested revisions:

a. Joanna's pet fish has more fins than her boyfriend's.
b. Jake walks his own dog more often than his son's.
c. Celia wants a vacation more than her fiancé does.
d. Correct
e. The review said the famous director's new movie was more violent than his last one.

46–1 RELATIVE CLAUSES AND RELATIVE PRONOUNS, page 78

a. We ordered trophies for all the players who we feel deserve recognition.
b. We always prefer to debate with people who express themselves forcefully.
c. Runners who stretch before they run have fewer injuries than those who don't stretch.
d. Correct
e. One of the violinists who play in the pops orchestra will be selected to join the symphony orchestra at the end of the season.

46–2 RELATIVE CLAUSES AND RELATIVE PRONOUNS, page 80

a. My mother, who has worked all her life, will finally retire in July.
b. The paper that we were assigned on October 10 is due on November 10.
c. The word *awesome,* which I use all the time, does not really mean "interesting" or "cool."
d. The counselor to whom I referred my brother was kind enough to find time in her schedule for him.
e. Students who study every day fare better on tests than students who cram the night before.

47–1 COMMAS: COORDINATION, INTRODUCTORY ELEMENTS, page 82

a. Unlike the national security adviser, the senator believed that the president needed a full accounting of events.
b. She does not know who her secret admirer is, but she appreciates the attention.
c. Wearing a beaded collar, the poodle pranced around the ring.
d. After mowing and trimming, the lawn looked like a velvet carpet.
e. Correct

47–2 COMMAS: NONRESTRICTIVE ELEMENTS AND TRANSITIONAL EXPRESSIONS, page 84

a. Alaska, the forty-ninth state, and Hawaii, the fiftieth, were both admitted to the Union in 1959.
b. We continue to assert, however, that dogs abandoned by their owners should first be offered to the public for adoption.
c. John Wesley Powell, who led geological expeditions into Colorado and Utah, had lost an arm during the Civil War.
d. Nevertheless, he decided to brave the storm and drive home.
e. Correct

47–3 COMMAS: MISCELLANEOUS USES, page 85

a. It was a hot, smoggy, and depressing day.
b. I opened the door, looked around the room, and finally spotted the raincoat I'd forgotten.
c. December 7, 1941, was the date that President Roosevelt said would "live in infamy."
d. Correct
e. Joan Bergmann, LL.D., opened her solo office as soon as she graduated from law school.

47–4 COMMAS: MISUSES, page 87

a. We should not necessarily think that he is the one to blame.
b. Eleven very tired Brownies and their adult leaders were happy to go home after the overnight camping trip.

c. Correct
d. Dixie, Peanuts, and Clement were what we called the puppies.
e. There are too many tomatoes in the soup and not enough carrots.

48–1 APOSTROPHES, page 89

a. I'll sew the costumes if you'll paint the sets.
b. Sarah liked to look at her brothers' record album covers from the '60s.
c. My sister-in-law's house is more than 150 years old; its most interesting feature is a hidden passageway in the library.
d. When we visited Ireland, we tried to locate the Murphys, who used to live next door to us.
e. Their house is on the sunny side of the street; ours is on the shady side.

49–1 QUOTATION MARKS, page 90

a. Why were we assigned Poe's story "The Tell-Tale Heart"?
b. The judge asked whether the jury had reached a verdict.
c. Our parents used to think that lyrics like "I want to hold your hand" were profound.
d. "I think that I shall never see / A billboard lovely as a tree," Ogden Nash wrote, in parody of Joyce Kilmer's poem "Trees."
e. The teacher asked, "Who said, 'Give me liberty or give me death'?"

50–1 SEMICOLONS, page 92

Suggested revisions:

a. Mary has lived in many places: Worcester, Massachusetts; Newark, New Jersey; Charleston, South Carolina; and Miami, Florida.
b. It snowed very little that winter; nevertheless, sales of ski equipment soared.
c. True friends exhibit four main qualities: openness, trust, loyalty, and love.
d. The county's water shortage was severe. Many restaurants in the area stopped serving water with meals unless a customer specifically requested it.
e. Correct

51–1 PERIODS, QUESTION MARKS, AND EXCLAMATION POINTS, page 94

a. Would you please give me a call as soon as you're ready?
b. "Are you crazy?" he asked.
c. "The tornado is heading straight for us!" he screamed. "Run for your life!"
d. My younger sister spent a week at a space camp run by NASA.
e. With parents like that, is it any wonder that he's always late?

51–2 COLONS, page 95

Suggested revisions:

a. His plan was obvious: break the window, cut the wires, snatch the jewels, and sneak down the fire escape.
b. My favorite Gospel story is that of the Samaritan woman at the well in John 4:9–30.
c. For her driving test, Monica hoped for a kind inspector, no yellow lights, no oncoming traffic, and no empty parking spots for parallel parking.
d. John was ready to go to his job interview, but there was one small problem: he couldn't find his car keys.
e. Correct

51–3 DASHES, PARENTHESES, BRACKETS, SLASHES, AND ELLIPSIS DOTS, page 97

Suggested revisions:

a. Vice President Richard Nixon (who later became the thirty-seventh president) said he was through with politics in his famous "Checkers" speech.
b. The judge said, "You [the defendant] are a menace to society."
c. His home run—what a blast!—made it over the center field fence in record time.
d. The monetary part of the award ($50) wasn't nearly as important as the recognition.
e. In her last speech to Torvald, Nora declares her independence: "I'm freeing you from being responsible. . . . There has to be absolute freedom for us both" (64).

52–1 UNDERLINING (ITALICS), page 99

a. The French use the term *bon appetit* at the beginning of a meal; many Americans now say simply, "Enjoy."

b. The poem "Song of Myself" appears in Walt Whitman's collection *Leaves of Grass.*

c. My two-year-old uses the word *dog* to refer to any animal.

d. Most Americans know the Latin word for *tree,* which is *arbor.*

e. I've seen the movie *Cinema Paradiso* four times, and I intend to see it at least four more.

53–1 CAPITALIZATION, page 100

a. Correct

b. The Republican Party was known as the antislavery party at the time of the Civil War.

c. During fall semester our architecture class visited Rockefeller Center, the Empire State Building, and St. Patrick's Cathedral.

d. Mahatma Gandhi applied the principles of civil disobedience to his struggle for Indian independence.

e. Virginia Cusack, executive vice president, was known to most of the workers as Ginny.

54–1 ABBREVIATIONS, page 101

a. Dr. Ruth Mullen was my pediatrician, and now she is my children's.

b. The students wondered how they would get through all of chapter 5 in one night.

c. Correct

d. The men voted to stay overnight in New York City, but the women voted to continue on to Philadelphia.

e. The FBI, the CIA, and the IRS don't have the best reputations with the American public.

55–1 NUMBERS, page 102

a. On 7 December 1941, Japanese planes attacked Pearl Harbor.

b. Correct

c. To get ready for the race, Yvonne ran three miles one day, five miles the next, and eight miles the next.

d. Nell took exactly $1.27 from her piggy bank when she went to the candy store.

e. Twelve times this year I've asked my neighbors to keep their dog tied up during the day when they're at work.

56–1 HYPHENATION, page 103

a. After the accident, Jake was semiconscious, and it took him forty-five minutes to remember his own name.

b. Three-quarters of the way through the test, I realized I didn't remember enough about post-Reconstruction America to answer the last essay question.

c. The short-term profit was a relief to the fledgling CEO.

d. Her way-out ideas have led to some really innovative advances in medical treatment.

e. The half-price items at the yard sale included a gas-powered leaf blower.

58–1 SPELLING, page 104

a. Gertrude was very embarrassed when her pocketbook spilled open on the subway train.

b. Most young people want independence from their parents, but many of them also want their parents to continue to support them, if only emotionally.

c. Correct

d. My sociology professor is very knowledgeable, but sometimes her knowledge interferes with common sense.

e. Our seventh-grade teacher always told us that our grammar was good but that we misspelled too much.

58–2 SPELLING, page 106

a. leaves
b. perceive
c. offered
d. Correct
e. prettiest

60–1 CATEGORIES OF NOUNS AND NOUN PLURALS, page 107

a. Westminster Abbey is one of the oldest churches in England. P: Westminster Abbey, England; CC: churches.
b. Many people believe they have been abducted by aliens from space. CC: people, aliens; UC: space.
c. Times Square has experienced a renaissance in recent years. P: Times Square; UC: renaissance; CC: years.
d. The *New York Times* employs many excellent reporters. P: *New York Times;* CC: reporters.
e. Jell-O is a brand of gelatin frequently used in making low-fat desserts. P: Jell-O; UC: gelatin; CC: desserts.

60–2 NOUNS AND ARTICLES, page 108

a. The line of tourists at the White House was already quite long, winding along the street next to the White House lawn toward the Ellipse.
b. I walked around the Ellipse and up a small hill to the Washington Monument.
c. The line there was not as long, so I waited underneath the circle of fifty flags, one for every state in the United States.
d. From information in my guidebook, I learned that the monument is 555 feet tall and was the tallest structure in the world when it was built in 1886.
e. From the observation area at the top of the monument I could see all of Washington spread out before me.

60–3 NOUNS AND ARTICLES, page 110

Suggested revisions:

a. I put a potato in the oven and then went out to the store. An hour later I had to phone my sister and ask her to take the potato out of the oven.
b. Money can't buy happiness, but it can pay the grocery bill.
c. Which country in South America is your roommate from?
d. Jorge asked his mother for advice about living away from home for the first time.
e. She ordered a hamburger and fries. The fries were delivered first; by the time the hamburger arrived at her table, she was finished eating all the fries.

61–1   THE *BE* AUXILIARY, page 112

Suggested revisions:

a. They are eating now.
b. The pool was drained last month.
c. The skyscraper was built in only three months.
d. Correct
e. June has been dieting for six weeks.

61–2   MODAL AUXILIARY VERBS, page 113

Suggested answers:

a. should sleep
b. must have locked
c. would have set
d. must wash
e. could, get

61–3   VERBS FOLLOWED BY AN INFINITIVE OR *-ING* VERBAL, page 115

a. The principal ordered the tardy student to stay after school every day for a week.
b. The committee discussed adopting the proposal but postponed voting on it until the next meeting.
c. On her first trip to Hawaii, she could not imagine being in a more beautiful place on earth.
d. Tony persuaded his mother to allow him to take the family car overnight.
e. We can no longer pretend to be uninvolved.

61–4   VERBALS USED AS ADJECTIVES, page 117

a. I am always annoyed by my little brother's early morning noise when I am trying to sleep late.
b. The statistics on underage drinking and driving are very depressing.
c. Sarah reluctantly brought her disappointing first-semester report card home to her parents.

d. The worried director made her exhausted cast run through the play one more time.
e. We couldn't imagine a more boring lecture, but we kept ourselves amused by passing notes across the back row.

62–1 SENTENCE STRUCTURE, page 118

Suggested revisions:

a. The committee sent a subpoena to the alleged witness.
b. Professor Moran explained exponential functions to the class.
c. Correct
d. The meteorology students visited Mount Washington yesterday.
e. Bob ran every morning because it helped him keep in shape.

62–2 DIRECT AND INDIRECT QUOTATIONS AND QUESTIONS, page 119

Suggested revisions:

a. During the inquiry, he kept repeating that he didn't see a thing.
b. The woman at the garden shop told us to plant the impatiens in a shady corner of the flowerbed.
c. She asked if I wanted to taste the brownies. I said sure, that I wanted to taste them.
d. My cousin asked if I remembered the summer we spent on Granddad's farm.
e. As she stepped out of the car at the airport terminal, Carla told her father not to bother, that she could handle her bags herself.

63–1 IDIOMATIC STRUCTURES, page 120

a. The dissatisfied passenger wrote a letter complaining about the lack of food on the four-hour train trip.
b. She has always been interested in archaeology.
c. When we arrived in Florence, we weren't sure whether to go to the Duomo or the Uffizi first.
d. He was content with his low-paying entry-level job because it left him time for his real passion: scuba diving.
e. We can't blame our parents for everything that happens to us in life.

63–2 IDIOMATIC STRUCTURES, page 122

Suggested revisions:

a. My cousin told me to look him up if I was ever in Idaho.
b. Correct
c. The team members counted on the high-scoring forward to make up for their shaky defense.
d. Whenever she lists the seven capital sins, she leaves out sloth.
e. The students were looking forward to traveling to Washington during spring break.